For Alex

Accountability FOR LEARNING

How Teachers and School Leaders Can Take Charge

DOUGLAS B. REEVES

Association for Supervision and Curriculum Development
Alexandria, Virginia USA

Association for Supervision and Curriculum Development
1703 N. Beauregard St. Alexandria, VA 22311-1714 USA
Telephone: 800-933-2723 or 703-578-9600 Fax: 703-575-5400
Web site: http://www.ascd.org E-mail: member@ascd.org
Author guidelines: www.ascd.org/write

Gene R. Carter, Executive Director; Nancy Modrak, Director of Publishing; Julie Houtz, Director of Book Editing & Production; Deborah Siegel, Project Manager; Shelley Young, Senior Graphic Designer; Jim Beals, Typesetter; Dina Seamon, Production Specialist.

Printed in the United States of America.

ASCD Member Book, No. FY04-4 (January 2004, PC). ASCD Member Books mail to Premium (P), Comprehensive (C), and Regular (R) members on this schedule: Jan., PC; Feb., P; Apr., PCR; May, P; July, PC; Aug., P; Sept., PCR; Nov., PC; Dec., P.

Paperback ISBN: 0-87120-833-4 • ASCD product #104004

Also available as an e-book through ebrary, netLibrary, and many online booksellers (see Books in Print for the ISBNs).

Library of Congress Cataloging-in-Publication Data
Reeves, Douglas B., 1953—
    Accountability for learning : how teachers and school leaders can take charge / Douglas Reeves.
        p. cm.
Includes bibliographical references and index.
    ISBN 0-87120-833-4 (alk. paper)
    1. Educational accountability--United States. 2. School improvement programs--United States. I. Association for Supervision and Curriculum Development. II. Title.

    LB2806.22.R44 2004
    379.1'58--dc22
                                                        2003022597

13 12 11 10 09 08 07   12 11 10 9 8 7 6 5 4 3 2

Accountability
FOR LEARNING

How Teachers and School Leaders Can Take Charge

Acknowledgments

My first debt is to the thousands of teachers, leaders, board members, writers, policymakers, and colleagues who have been willing to engage me on the issues of educational accountability. Because they take the time and invest the energy to challenge me with their provocative insights and demands for practical solutions, I have been forced to reexamine my assumptions, admit my mistakes, and eat more than one slice of humble pie. They jolt me out of the ivory tower and confront me daily with the realities of financial crises, burned-out staff, and unmotivated students, parents, and even some educators. Amid these doses of unpleasant reality, they also provide compelling case studies of success in the most unlikely places. Just as their candor challenges me, their stories of success give me energy, hope, and enthusiasm.

This book marks my first collaboration with ASCD, a publisher that has brought to educators around the world some of the most important books of the last several decades. I am honored to be in their company. As always, Esmond Harmsworth of the Zachary Shuster Harmsworth Literary Agency attended to every detail to make this partnership work smoothly.

Footnotes and reference listings are sadly inadequate ways to acknowledge the intellectual debt that I owe to many leading thinkers in this field. I have in particular been influenced by the following scholars, some of whom are cited in this volume, and the rest of whom influence my writing in ways that extend far beyond a footnote: Anne Bryant, Lucy McCormick Calkins, Linda Darling-Hammond, Daniel Goleman, Audrey Kleinsasser, Robert Marzano, Alan Moore, Mike Schmoker, and Grant Wiggins.

My colleagues at the Center for Performance Assessment are part of every project for which I receive credit far out of proportion to my own contribution. For this book, I am particularly indebted to Cathy Shulkin, whose work on the appendices and references were essential to the timely completion of the project. How she did this while balancing a thousand details of my professional life is a mystery, but I suspect it has a lot to do with intelligence, commitment, and an extraordinary work ethic. Larry Ainsworth, Eileen Allison, Arlana Bedard, Jan Christinson, Donna Davis, Cheryl Dunkle, Tony Flach, Michele LePatner, Dave Nagel, Elaine Robbins-Harris, Stacy Scott, Earl Shore, Jill Unziker-Lewis, Mike White, Steve White, Nan Woodson, and my other colleagues at the Center have contributed not only to my thinking about accountability but to my daily intellectual growth. Anne Fenske, the Center's executive director, and our colleagues deliver more than a thousand professional development engagements every year for hundreds of thousands of educators and school leaders. My sincere thanks go to Sarah Abrahamson, Greg Atkins, Ken Bingenheimer, Melissa Blunden, Nan Caldwell, Laura Davis, Angie Hodapp, Matt Minney, and Dee Ruger.

My family loves and supports me through teaching, travel, preoccupation, and exhaustion. James, Julia, Brooks, and Shelley forgive my absences and indulge my passion for kids, schools, and books. Alex, to whom this book is dedicated, celebrates his 16th birthday as my 16th book goes to press. He plays the guitar and is more cool than is probably legal in the state of Massachusetts. At that age I had a pocket protector with a leaking pen, black plastic glasses, and "cool" was a climatic term. He is also a generous and decent young man, a fabulous big brother, and a *mensch* of whom his family is very proud.

Douglas Reeves
Swampscott, Massachusetts

Introduction

Teachers and educational leaders are extraordinarily busy, inundated with demands for more work and better results with fewer resources—and less time. You will decide within the next few paragraphs whether this book is worth your time. Let me come straight to the point. *Accountability for Learning* equips teachers and leaders with the ability to transform educational accountability policies from destructive and demoralizing accounting drills into meaningful and constructive decision making in the classroom, school, and district. You do not need to wait for new changes in federal or state legislation. This book is about what you can do right now to improve learning, teaching, and leadership. Although I respect the role that senior leaders, board members, and policymakers play in education (see Chapter 6), the plain fact is that accountability for learning happens in the classroom.

The traditional failures in educational accountability are not born of a lack of knowledge or will. We know what to do, yet decades of research and reform have failed to connect leadership

1

intentions to classroom reality. This "knowing-doing gap" (Pfeffer & Sutton, 2000) is hardly unique to education. Businesses, nonprofit organizations, health care agencies, and religious institutions all suffer from the breach between intention and reality. The cause is neither indifference nor indolence, yet many initiatives begin with those assumptions. If only the presentation is persuasive enough, if only the rewards are great enough, if only the sanctions are tough enough, the reasoning goes, then the staff will see the light and they will at last comply with the wishes of those giving instructions. If sincere intentions were sufficient for success, then the landscape of educational reform would not be littered with frustrated leaders and policymakers who noticed that, after rendering a decision about something that seemed momentous, absolutely nothing happened in the classroom. The board adopted academic standards and solemnly vowed that all children would meet them. Nothing happened in the classroom. The superintendent announced a new vision statement, along with core values and an organizational mission that the entire staff would enthusiastically chant. Nothing happened in the classroom. Millions were spent on new technology. Nothing happened in the classroom. Staff development programs were adopted so that teachers, like circus animals, would be "trained" to perform new feats. Although seats were dutifully warmed during countless trainings, nothing happened in the classroom. Frustrated by these organizational failures, policymakers finally got tough and decided that accountability was the answer. School systems and individual buildings were rated, ranked, sorted, and humiliated. Sanctions, including job loss or reassignment, and rewards, including thousands of dollars in bonuses, were offered as alternating sticks and carrots, as accountability policies were reduced to artlessly wielded blunt instruments. Yet despite the rhetoric, threats, and promises, nothing happened in the classroom.

This book is not about achieving compliance through a combination of threat and guile. Rather, this book begins with the fundamental premise that educators and school leaders want to be successful. Moreover, these professionals are more than a little weary at the prospect of implementing one more program, particularly when it is placed on top of other "proven" programs within the same time constraints. What this book provides is not an external prescription for success, but rather a method for creating your own prescriptions based on your own data, your own observations, and your own documentation of your most effective practices. Oscar Wilde exaggerated only slightly when he said, "Education is an admirable thing, but it is well to remember from time to time that nothing that is worth knowing can be taught." This does not mean that I reject external research and formal study. On the contrary, I rely heavily on the foundational work of such leading scholars as Robert Marzano (2003) and his groundbreaking synthesis of 35 years of educational research. My colleagues at the Center for Performance Assessment and I have tried to contribute a few pebbles to the mountain of research on school effectiveness. But without application in the classroom, our efforts are in vain.

Two paths lead to the effective application of research. The first is ham-handed prescription in which the carefully nuanced ideas of researchers become mutated into the delivery of a script, an enterprise that would be much more successful were it not for the inconvenient involvement of humans. The second is a process of inquiry, discovery, and personal application. In the first process, teachers in exasperation say, "Just tell us what to do!" In the second process, teachers say, "Let's try it, test it, reflect on it, and refine it. We need to make this work for our students and we need to recognize that this is a school, not a factory." Thus this book introduces "student-centered accountability" as a constructive alternative to the data gathering and reporting systems that now masquerade as educational accountability.

A fair question is why teachers should be involved in accountability at all. After all, isn't educational accountability something that is traditionally "done to" teachers? Their role, tradition has it, is to carry out the orders of the central office. Here is the great irony: more real accountability occurs when teachers actively participate in the development, refinement, and reporting of accountability. Call it the prescription paradox. Leaders engage in prescription because they believe that it will create greater accountability. In fact, the greater the prescription, the less real accountability that ensues. "Sure, we'll do it," the teachers respond. But they implement the prescription with neither enthusiasm nor engagement. The students require mere nanoseconds to pick up on the uncertainty and cynicism of some of the most trusted adults in their lives, the teachers. Less prescription surely suggests a risk. Without prescription, variation will occur, as well as inconsistencies and personal judgments. The absence of prescription will also allow moments of discovery, enthusiasm, dedication, sharing of successes, and relentless persistence despite extraordinary challenges. The flip side of the prescription paradox is that with less prescription, there is genuine accountability. There is, in a phrase, accountability for learning.

1

The "A-Word": Why People Hate Accountability and What You Can Do About It

For many educators, *accountability* has become a dirty word. One superintendent even admonished me not to use "the A-word" because it was just too emotionally volatile a term in his district. No wonder. In virtually every school system in the world, accountability is little more than a litany of test scores. The prevailing presumption is that test scores, typically reported as the averages of classes, schools, or systems, are the only way to hold teachers accountable. Teachers know, of course, that their jobs are far more complex than what can be measured by students' performance on a single test, and they understandably resent the simplistic notion that their broad curriculum, creative energy, and attention to the needs of individual students can be summed up with a single number.

As educators, we have two choices. We can rail against the system, hoping that standards and testing are a passing fad, or we can lead the way in a fundamental reformulation of educational accountability. We can wait for policymakers to develop holistic accountability plans (Reeves, 2002b), or we can be proactive in exceeding the requirements of prevailing accountability systems. The central thesis of this book is that if teachers embrace account-ability, they can profoundly influence educational policy for the better. If teachers systematically examine their professional prac-tices and their impact on student achievement, the results of such reflective analysis will finally transform educational accountability from a destructive and unedifying mess to a constructive and transformative force in education.

Student-Centered Accountability

In the following chapters, we explore how student-centered ac-countability is fundamentally different from traditional models that rely exclusively on test scores. The terms "student-centered account-ability" or "holistic accountability" refer to a system that includes not only academic achievement scores, but also specific information on curriculum, teaching practices, and leadership practices. In addition, a student-centered system includes a balance of quantitative and qualitative indicators—the story behind the numbers. Finally, stu-dent-centered accountability focuses on the progress of individual students and does not rely exclusively on averages of large groups of students who may or may not share similar learning needs, teaching strategies, attendance patterns, and other variables that influence test performance. Note that student-centered accountability does not *ex-clude* test scores but places the traditional accountability reports in context. Only when community leaders, board members, administra-tors, parents, and teachers understand the context of accountability can they understand the meaning of the numbers that now adorn the educational box scores of local newspapers.

The immediate challenge to student-centered accountability is typically expressed by those who say, "But the public won't listen to anything but the scores—no one is interested in anything but the bottom line!" Fortunately, recent events have provided a compelling rejoinder to this logic. The corporate debacles of the early 21st cen-tury provide powerful evidence to support the thesis that single num-bers—the proverbial "bottom line"—do not tell the whole story in business any better than they do in education. Every teacher knows that the presentation of data without a deep understanding of underlying causes is analytically bankrupt. After all, Enron had great numbers, and now legions of would-be retirees regret that they did not better understand the story behind the numbers. Corporate financial disclosures that include multiple measures and narratives as well as numbers are likely to be more useful than the publication of box scores. In the context of education, the "educational Enron" will occur when a school receives short-term praise for higher test scores and only later is it revealed that the school had an exceptionally high dropout rate among students who might have underperformed on the test and an exceptionally high ratio of students who were classified as special education and were excluded from testing.

Teachers should take the lead in redefining and improving educational accountability for three essential reasons. First, child-centered accountability is more accurate than traditional accountability. Second, it is more constructive. And third, it is better for motivation of faculty and staff members.

More Accurate

To understand why child-centered accountability is more accurate than traditional accountability, consider a medical analogy. My teenage daughter needs to lose 20 pounds, the doctor advises. Within a few weeks, my daughter proudly announces, "Dad, I've lost 20 pounds!" Can we be satisfied that this measurement—lost weight—is an accurate portrayal of my daughter's health? I don't think so. We might have one conclusion if we take the time to learn that her weight loss is the result of diet and exercise, and we might come to a strikingly different conclusion if we discover that the weight loss is due to drug abuse and an eating disorder. The "score"—the loss of 20 pounds—is the same, but the score is not an accurate reflection of the health of the patient without the additional information we might gain from "patient-centered" accountability. Similarly, high or low test scores tell us little of value if we do not have the context provided by student-centered accountability.

More Constructive

Student-centered accountability is more constructive than traditional accountability because it focuses on the improvement of teaching and learning rather than merely rendering an evaluation and the publication of a report. What, after all, is the fundamental purpose of classroom assessment? Is it merely the announcement of a grade and the classification of the student? In the most successful classes, teachers and students understand that the purpose of assessment is the improvement of student performance. We test so that we know how to learn better and how to teach better. When a test reflects inadequate performance, the result is not merely a score, but a process of improvement. The purpose of educational accountability is also the improvement of teaching and learning. It is a constructive process in which successful results can be associated with specific teaching and leadership practices so that teachers and leaders can be recognized and their successful practices can be replicated. When an accountability system displays inadequate results, the purpose is not humiliation and accusation, but an intentional search for the underlying causes of poor achievement and the development of specific strategies for improvement. Every teacher I know wants students to be successful—it's just a more fun way to live, and student success provides the motivation for our persistence in a challenging and complex profession. We have a much higher probability of engagement in a process of continuous improvement for ourselves and for our students when we have an accountability system that is oriented toward constructive understanding of improvement rather than one that is limited to an announcement of a judgment about our failures.

Better for Motivation

The third reason that student-centered accountability is an imperative for today's schools is that it is far better for the morale, motivation, and engagement of faculty and staff members. The importance of staff engagement cannot be overstated; the independent, voluntary activities of staff members are far more related to organizational success than mere compliance with administrative mandates (Coffman, Gonzalez Molina, & Clifton, 2002). No matter how structured the curriculum or tightly managed the school day, the interactions between students and teachers are to a large extent the result of the individual diligence, professionalism, and commitment of teachers. Even the most peripatetic administrator cannot be in every classroom all the time, supervising the instructional process. Moreover, the most detailed accountability processes cannot ensure high-quality instruction without high levels of teacher commitment to and engagement in the process. High levels of teacher dissatisfaction with traditional accountability processes are reflected in widespread reports of teacher stress, anxiety, and resentment, sometimes inaccurately reported as an unwillingness of teachers to be accountable at all. An important source of the resulting teacher disengagement is a sense of futility and a lack of control over the accountability process. In my interviews with teachers throughout the United States, a significant theme recurs: teachers are willing to be accountable, but they find it frustrating in the extreme to be held accountable for students who do not attend school, and they are angry that teachers and principals are the only people in the system who are held accountable, when other participants in the child's education, including parents, support staff, and central office administrators, also have important roles to play in the achievement of educational results.

Although it is certainly not a panacea for teacher and staff discouragement, student-centered accountability can nevertheless restore to teachers a degree of confidence in the fairness and meaning of educational accountability because it includes indicators that can be directly controlled and influenced by teachers. Moreover, because student-centered accountability is comprehensive and includes more than test scores, such a system makes clear the importance of teacher quality, parent involvement, student mobility, and a host of other factors that are ignored or obscured in traditional accountability reports.

Student-centered accountability is not a public relations exercise, showing only the successes of schools and covering up the failures. But student-centered accountability does provide careful documentation of success at the classroom level, including many successes that are overlooked in a recitation of average test scores. Because it includes a balance of quantitative and qualitative mea- surements, student-centered accountability will include the stories, case studies, and vignettes that define great teaching and leader- ship. Moreover, the accumulation of hundreds and thousands of these case studies provides a research base for the systematic iden- tification of what works in each school and district. Staff morale is improved dramatically not through false affirmation—"Everything is fine!" when in fact it is manifestly clear that everything is not fine. Rather, staff morale is improved when challenges are faced honestly and leaders recognize that many of the solutions for confronting those challenges are in their own school and district. Great leaders develop systematic ways to catch teachers doing things right, docu- ment those successes, make those successes the focal point of fac- ulty meetings and professional development sessions, and leverage those successes when confronting failures and challenges. These practices are the difference between teachers who say, "We have problems, and it's hopeless—it's the fault of the kids and families" and the teachers who say, "We have problems, and our examination of the evidence tells us that we also have solutions, and here is how we will address each challenge . . ."

Teacher Leadership in Accountability

When accountability is the exclusive initiative of the legislature, the board of education, or the superintendent, the inevitable conse- quence is the perception that accountability is something "done to" students and teachers. Even in those schools and districts where leaders pride themselves on a culture of "shared decision making" or "site-based management," the creation and implementation of accountability systems is a frequent exception that undermines every leadership initiative. This inconsistency provides ample ammunition to the cynics who complain of the superintendent, "Sure, she talks a good game about participative decision making, but when it came time to design the accountability system, it was strictly top-down management. The leader's actions made clear that teacher opinions didn't matter and that our feedback was irrelevant." To be fair, many superintendents would respond, "But my hands are tied—I'm only doing what the state legislature and my school board are making me do." There is a way out of this impasse, and that is teacher leadership in educational accountability.

When it comes to rewarding teachers, I have frequently told school boards and superintendents, "There are no laws that prevent you from paying teachers more than you have agreed to pay." Conversely, there are no laws that prevent teachers from being more accountable than state laws and district policies require. Perhaps your school system is mired in the trap in which educational accountability is simply a set of test scores. Rather than wait for the legislature, the school board, or the superintendent to change, why not take the lead? Even in the most primitive accountability environment, teachers can take the lead by analyzing their own practices and testing the relationship of those practices to student achievement. Even when senior leaders resist student-centered accountability, teachers can exercise their choices in professional development and assert their prerogatives in faculty meetings, department meetings, and grade-level meetings by focusing on their impact on student achievement. Teachers can produce newsletters and accountability reports that tell the story behind the numbers and communicate with parents and other stakeholders about their challenges and success stories. Teachers can produce "best practices" books that frankly acknowledge their mistakes and highlight their successes, providing guidance for new teachers and veterans alike. Teachers can, in a word, embrace accountability. They can approach their leaders, their school board, and the public, saying, "We are going to be more accountable than you asked us to be, and we are going to do accountability in a way that is constructive and student-centered. We don't have to do this by virtue of any law or policy, but we are choosing to do so because it is the right thing to do and it is in the best interests of the children we serve."

If this vision of accountability sounds appealing, then read the following chapters to learn how to do it. If it sounds impossible, then read the following chapters to learn how your colleagues across the country have already done it. If it sounds complicated, then read the following chapters to discover some tools that you can use immediately to demystify the complexities of assessments and accountability. Although student-centered accountability is not easy, it is infinitely more rewarding than the prevailing model of test scores, threats, intimidation, and poisoned morale. The effort you invest in this process will be rewarded in better student achievement, improved professional practices, greater personal satisfaction, and more fun every day in the world's most important job.

2

Accountability Essentials: Identifying and Measuring Teaching Practices

Mrs. Hadzel was near tears as she looked at the article on the front page of the local newspaper. It listed, for all the world to see, the recent test scores of every classroom in every school in the community. Steadfastly refusing to bend to the forces of time and declining eyesight, she eschewed bifocals. But for this article, the small print in the newspaper required her to resort to a magnifying glass. There she was: "4H Stanley 82 Sat." The reader was supposed to discern that this meant that the students in her 4th grade class at Stanley Elementary School—denoted "H" because of the first letter of her last name—had scored an average of 82 on their composite scores on the most recent state examination and therefore were deemed "satisfactory."

"All that work, all that progress, all that love, and this is what people think I am—4H Stanley 82 Sat," she thought. "What about the parent meetings? What about the hours before and after school with Mikhail who didn't speak English when he came here but took the test anyway and scored in the 70s? What about Lamar who was developmentally delayed and, with some extra time, finished the entire test and beamed with pride as he put down his pencil, exhausted, after four hours and achieved a score of 36?" Mrs. Hadzel's pride in Lamar was particularly poignant because her own disabled daughter had been artfully excluded from the state test by a team of teachers and administrators who feared that she would bring down the school's test scores.

Why do we reduce the art and science of teaching to superficial numbers? The easy response is to blame a cabal of politicians and administrators or to expand the conspiracy theory to include big business and the entertainment industry. But the role of victim is unworthy of the teaching profession, and we must do better. Why has accountability been reduced to a litany of test scores? Because we have failed to tell our story. Because we have, in fact, resisted many attempts to measure classroom activities, professional teaching strategies, curriculum implementation, and building-based leadership decisions. We insisted that "teaching is an art, not a science" and that we were therefore impervious to scrutiny and accurate measurement. That gave our critics the easy choice of reducing the Mrs. Hadzels of the world to "4H Stanley 82 Sat."

It need not be this way. Educational accountability can be holistic rather than fragmentary. Accountability can tell the story of the students, teachers, administrators, parents, and partnerships that make their schools no less than places of wonder. This is not a wistful hope from the ivory tower, but a conclusion reached after direct observation of teachers committed to making accountability more than test scores.

Teachers across the nation have already begun to create new accountability systems that reflect not only the effects of their work, but also the causes of student achievement. One would think that their efforts would be welcomed, but in fact they have had to overcome a torrent of opposition from those who, while complaining about tests, also resist the use of any other accountability mechanism. The critics of holistic accountability feed into the public education critics who revel in the rhetoric that states that educators are unaccountable and intransigent. Only test scores, the critics claim, will whip the lazy teachers into shape. By such logic, the critics would conduct blood pressure tests for patients with hypertension but pay no attention to diet, exercise, pharmaceuticals, or hereditary diseases—all they would care about is the blood pressure test score. That is hardly an illuminating exercise for the patient, but if hypertensive patients were as attractive targets as public education, then few people would find such silly and illogical analysis annoying. If educators are to make the case that accountability is more than test scores, then they must embrace, rather than resist, accountability as a constructive force. Educators must tell their story, including the extraordinary efforts they make on behalf of students and parents every day. This will require a combination of a quantitative measurement of their daily activities and a qualitative description of their intensity, intellect, and commitment. In other words, they must embrace holistic accountability.

Components of Holistic Accountability

I have described the central thesis that "accountability is more than test scores" in two other books: *Accountability in Action: A Blueprint for Learning Organizations* (Reeves, 2000a) and *Holistic Accountability: Serving Students, Schools, and Community* (Reeves, 2002b). *Accountability in Action* provides a step-by-step method for a team of administrators and teachers to create a comprehensive district accountability system. *Holistic Accountability* is a much shorter introduction to the nature of holistic accountability and is appropriate as an overview for board members, legislators, and senior administrators. How is the book you are now reading different? This book focuses on the needs of teachers. It does not depend upon new accountability policies by state legislators or the local board of education. Rather, it focuses on steps that can be taken at the building and classroom levels to transform educational accountability from a destructive force into a constructive approach to the improvement of teaching and learning. Even in states and school systems that remain mired in the myth that educational accountability is nothing more than a set of test scores, effective teachers can, on their own initiative, begin to reframe accountability so that they provide essential context for those scores. This context includes the rich description of teaching, curriculum, student actions, and leadership decisions. This context is what makes accountability make sense.

The Antecedents of Excellence

There are two types of educators reading this book. An educator in the first group might say, "I know I'm good and I know that my students have high achievement. They always look great when the district and state accountability scores come out, so why should I bother doing any additional work on accountability? This 'holistic accountability' stuff just sounds like more paperwork to me, and I'd rather spend that time interacting with my students." An educator in the second group might lament, "I'm exhausted—no matter how hard I work and no matter what I do, there is little relationship between the effort I put into my profession and the results that the newspaper publishes about our test scores. This is little wonder— more than 40 percent of the kids who took the state test in the spring were not here in the fall, and I have colleagues for whom mobility is an even bigger problem—80 percent of the kids who take the state test were not with the teacher all year long either because of mobility or because of excessive absences. How can those scores reflect our abilities as professional educators?"

Both of these groups of educators deserve a thoughtful response. To the first group I would say that if the present accountability system is working well for them, they should be exceptionally happy and appreciate their good fortune. It is rare indeed for a teacher to say that the local newspaper, not to mention the state or district accountability system, reflects the full extent of their efforts. Upon closer examination, even the most sanguine teacher will usually acknowledge those golden moments in the classroom when a connection is made with a student, the proficient student makes a leap to exceptional work, or the discouraged student becomes engaged. These moments, the ones that define our careers years after the students have moved along, are rarely evident in the sterile numbers that masquerade as accountability. Thus even the highly recognized teacher whose students' scores are high and who has not yet felt the political pressures of accountability should find a systematic emphasis on the

measurement of teaching, leadership, and curriculum a welcome improvement in the accountability system.

The second group of teachers—those who are working exceptionally hard but whose efforts receive scant recognition in the
prevailing accountability system—are the ones who will become
the fiercest advocates of holistic accountability. They know that
the scores of the typical accountability system do not reflect their
efforts any more than do the medical statistics of patients who
started to participate in a clinical trial but, as time went on, failed
to take their medication, moved on to another doctor, or deliberately engaged in counterproductive health behaviors. If the patients in those medical studies were children and the parents failed
to ensure that the children took their medications, avoided harm-
ful activities, and generally followed the physicians' instructions,
then the reviewers of the medical studies would be quick to acknowledge the effect of variables other than the skill of the doctor
and the quality of the hospital. When those patients inevitably
report adverse health effects, few people blame the doctor. Yet
when students who are absent, transient, inattentive, or unsup-
ported at home are included in the equation, then the low scores invariably lead to the inference that the teacher and the school system
have failed. There must be a better way.

As the analogy to medical studies makes clear, we must consider not only the effect variables—the health of the patients—but
also the cause variables—the actions of the physicians as well as the
actions of others who might influence patient health. In the context
of schools, the essence of holistic accountability is that we must
consider not only the effect variables—test scores—but also the
cause variables—the indicators in teaching, curriculum, parent involvement, leadership decisions, and a host of other factors that influence student achievement. Here teachers must make a
thoughtful commitment and resolve a prevailing dilemma. On the
one hand, teachers have been so burdened by tests and paperwork
that their visceral reaction to any additional burden is, "Enough! I'm
overworked already and simply do not have the time for one more
thing." If that reaction prevails against the requests for additional
documentation in holistic accountability, then we will play right into
the hands of our critics. Upon seeing a set of poor test scores, they

will say, "Sure, the teachers say that they have done all these other
things, but at the end of the day, the only real evidence we have is
right here—the evidence of test scores that show that the teachers
aren't doing the job."

The dilemma is clear. On the one hand, teachers say, "Accountability is much more than test scores—we should receive credit for
the extraordinary work that we do that is not measured in the typical accountability system!" On the other hand, many teachers say,
"Don't ask me for more reporting or paperwork—I'm exhausted
and burned out as it is." The only way out of this dilemma is to recognize that we are our own best advocates. Only by telling our
story, by providing qualitative and quantitative information on the
enormous amount of work that occurs in the classroom, can we
begin to balance the scales and bring some sense and logic to educational accountability. Only by providing additional data on curriculum and teaching practices can we provide context to the box
scores that now dominate the field of accountability.

Key Indicators in Holistic Accountability

Holistic accountability relies on key indicators that can be grouped
into four categories: (1) teaching, (2) leadership, (3) curriculum,
and (4) parent and community involvement. (See Appendix A for a
list of indicators used in an actual accountability system.)

Teaching

"Teaching is an art, not a science," a very angry union leader told
me. "What we do just can't be measured," she insisted. I stifled my
immediate impulse, which was to retort that the same argument was
made before the Renaissance about medicine. A physician of that
era might fail to wash his hands for days on end and dismiss any
consequences, such as dead patients, as the result of bad humors or
evil spirits. Systematic measurement challenged the physicians'
moral authority. Fortunately for us all, the scientific method ultimately prevailed. There remains, in the 21st century, an art to the

practice of medicine. That art includes the empathy and genuine concern that some physicians possess and others, using the same scientific protocols, do not. Nevertheless, we are lucky that even the impersonal and nonempathetic physicians rely on scientifically established procedures.

Similarly in education, my critic was right when she insisted that "teaching is an art." But acknowledging the art involved in the engagement of a child, in the genuine love and caring that is never reflected on a teaching test or a list of state scores, does not obviate this fact: repeated systematic observations tell us that certain teaching practices will, with a high degree of probability, have a positive effect on students. We know, for example, that accurate and timely feedback and the consistent requirement to represent complex ideas in different ways are techniques that are strongly associated with improved student performance (Marzano, Pickering, & Pollock, 2001). We also know that authentic assessments and nonfiction writing, accompanied by editing and rewriting, are strongly associated with improved student achievement (Calkins, 1994; Darling-Hammond, 1997; Reeves, 2000b).

The effective application of holistic accountability will identify ordinary teachers doing extraordinary things. Moreover, the accurate and consistent recording of these extraordinary efforts will make clear the value of identifying such efforts—even as students move from one school to another, even as some fail to attend school regularly, even as others arrive in school with remarkable social and learning deficits that are not remedied in a single year. Without such recording, teachers become the victims of a stereotype associated with their students' test scores. Holistic accountability, in brief, catches teachers doing things right. The following list provides a few teaching activities that might be appropriate to include in your consideration of holistic accountability.

- Frequency of writing assessment.
- Frequency of collaborative scoring.
- Percentage of agreement on scoring of anonymous student work.
- Time required to reach 80 percent consensus in scoring.
- Percentage of lessons integrating technology.

- Percentage of non–language arts lessons involving student writing with editing and rewriting.
- Frequency of feedback to students that results in their taking direct action based on that feedback.
- Frequency of updates in student writing portfolio.
- Frequency of updates in student reading assessment (Running Record or similar folder).
- Percentage of student portfolios receiving comparable evaluations by colleague or administrator.

Leadership

As a fundamental moral principle, no child in any school will be more accountable than the adults in the system. Similarly, it is a moral principle of leadership that no teacher or staff member will be more accountable than the leaders in the system. If we persist in maintaining accountability systems in which accountability is something "done to" students and teachers, then we will have failed to offer a morally sustainable policy.

A constructive alternative is available. In holistic accountability, leaders embrace the opportunity to be accountable. They identify various aspects of their approach to their work, such as specific behaviors in their coaching of colleagues, the way that they use their discretionary time, and the manner in which they implement their values. These behaviors can be observed in a measurable fashion and then reported with the same consistency and rigor as is the case with student test scores or teaching behaviors. The following is a partial list of potential leadership behaviors for you to consider as part of your holistic accountability system.

- Percentage of faculty meeting discussion and action items related to student achievement.
- Percentage of professional development activities directly related to classroom practice that is, in turn, related to student achievement.

- Percentage of parents who agree or strongly agree with the statement, "I feel welcome to visit my child's classroom at any time."
- Frequency of recognition of teacher best practices.
- Percentage of A-level tasks on daily prioritized task list directly related to improved student achievement.
- Percentage of faculty members with student achievement practices in assessment, curriculum, and instruction at the "distinguished" level according to a collaboratively scored rubric of professional practices.
- Percentage of certified staff members' available time devoted to student contact.
- Percentage of students with identified academic deficiencies who are rescheduled for additional assistance within 30 days of the identified need.
- Percentage of leader-initiated parent contacts related to academic achievement.

Curriculum

An extraordinary amount of work has gone into curriculum reform in the past several years. Many school systems have engaged in curriculum mapping, and virtually every school in the United States has attempted to ensure that its curriculum is aligned with relevant state standards. The work on these documents, however, does not allow for a single link to holistic accountability unless the school system is willing to measure and report the relationship of those curriculum efforts to actual implementation in the classroom. The following list provides some examples of how you can measure and use curriculum in a holistic accountability system.

- Percentage of students who are one or more grade levels below current grade in reading who receive targeted assistance.
- Percentage of classrooms that allow multiple opportunities for student success.

- Percentage of finals with failing grades that students may resubmit so that they have the potential for success.

- Percentage of students participating in advanced classes.

- Percentage of students participating in "pre-advanced" classes.

- Percentage of leader visits in which the actual classroom activity corresponds to the planned activity.

- Percentage of physical education classes incorporating academic content and assessment in writing, reading, mathematics, or science.

- Percentage of music classes incorporating academic content and assessment in writing, reading, mathematics, or social studies.

- Percentage of art classes incorporating academic content and assessment in writing, reading, mathematics, science, or social studies.

Parent and Community Involvement

"What about the other 18 hours of the day?" asked a teacher who wondered how that small portion of the day he was supposed to influence compared in impact with the time students spent at home, either under the tutelage of loving and attentive parents, or left to fend for themselves, or subject to a torrent of abuse. It was no surprise to this veteran educator that the same kids whose parents invariably volunteered for committees and regularly visited the classroom were also the ones whose backpacks were neat, whose homework was done, and whose "parent packets" received a meticulous inspection. Other children in the same class, by contrast, had been labeled "disorganized" or "lazy" or "inattentive" because their parents' duties ended with putting the child on the bus and their instruction at home was most likely to come from a television set. "Who am I grading, anyway—" the teacher wonders, "the student or the parent?"

The involvement of parents or other significant adults clearly has a major effect on student achievement. Although every teacher, school leader, educational policymaker, and parent knows this, the educational accountability systems on which we rely almost always fail to take into account the role of parents. Holistic accountability offers a better alternative. The following list describes meaningful ways to measure and report parent and community involvement.

- Multiple channels of parent communication are available, including the following:
  ✧ Face-to-face meetings at school,
  ✧ Personal meetings at nonschool locations,
  ✧ Incoming phone calls with personal response,
  ✧ Incoming phone calls with voicemail,
  ✧ School-initiated calls by teachers,
  ✧ School-initiated calls by administrators,
  ✧ School-initiated calls by other student advocates,
  ✧ Internet-based communication,
  ✧ E-mail initiated by parents,
  ✧ E-mail initiated by school, and
  ✧ Other channels of communication:
    – Student achievement results are communicated to parents with more information than letter grades.
    – Student achievement results for students in danger of failure are communicated at least every week to parents.
    – Student achievement results for students previously in danger of failure who are now demonstrating exceptional progress are communicated at least every week to parents.
- Teachers identify a "watch list" of students in danger of failure and a team approach, including parents, is used to monitor and improve student performance.
- Parents have multiple ways of becoming engaged in school support activities.
- More than 90 percent of students have a caring adult who regularly is involved in school support activities.

- Parents have the opportunity to participate in scoring student work using standards and scoring guides.

- Parent scoring of student work is comparable to teacher scoring of student work.

- Test information is sent to parents in a timely and understandable form.

- The community receives a comprehensive accountability report, including student achievement indicators as well as the "antecedents of excellence" involving teaching, leadership, and curriculum variables.

- Community communications include monthly success stories from schools featuring specific teachers and students.

- Community communications use multiple channels, including the following:

  ✧ Speaker's bureau of teachers, administrators, students, and parents,

  ✧ News releases,

  ✧ Publications created by students,

  ✧ Publications created by teachers and leaders,

  ✧ Television and/or radio broadcasts, and

  ✧ Internet-based communications, including Web site and e-mail.

- Community members with preschool children are invited to parent activities.

- Community members with children in home school and private school are invited to parent activities.

- Political leaders, business leaders, and community leaders are regularly invited for two-way interchanges with faculty members, leaders, students, and parents.

- Student academic success is showcased in the school's most prominent display areas, including trophy cases and hallways.

- The school recognizes student academic success with the same intensity as the community recognizes athletic success.

Framework or Micromanagement?

The lists of accountability indicators can be daunting, leading teachers to insist that Big Brother is watching their every move and to vigorously resist any attempt at measurement. In the current climate of accountability, however, we cannot have it both ways. Either we are reduced to a set of test scores or we seize the opportunity to tell the real story of educational accountability, sharing the subtleties and complexities of the world of teaching and learning.

Here is a cardinal principle of measurement: it is more important and accurate to measure a few things frequently and consistently than to measure many things once. Many school improvement plans, strategic plans, and accountability systems are annual events, in which reporting and analysis take place at the end of the year. In such systems, we repeat the same error of the typical state test that measures student performance once. The public then receives a somber report—many months later—that shows that the schools achieved or failed to achieve. By the time teachers receive the information, the students have moved on to the next grade, and a new set of challenges displaces any thoughtful reflection.

In the present controversies over accountability, the prevailing allegation is that test scores are "hard data," whereas teaching practices are "soft" and, by implication, less worthy. Such a dichotomy is unproductive and false. Test scores create the illusion of precision, but the best practice for teachers and leaders is to consider the preponderance of evidence, not a single score. Although great teaching is indeed an art, it is also subject to description, measurement, and, best of all, replication. Ours is a collaborative profession, and we do the cause no service by shrouding it in mystery or claiming that it cannot be measured or otherwise made subject to accountability. The things we most value we hold most accountable, and thus teachers and leaders should embrace, not resist, progressive accountability systems.

Holistic accountability does not provide a mechanism for classroom micromanagement. Rather, it provides a framework within which educational professionals can make many different logical choices. Based on the needs of one set of students, a teacher may choose to embrace innovative problem-solving techniques. Another group of students may benefit from a radical improvement in the frequency and specifics of teacher feedback. Yet another group of students may benefit from the systematic use of different educators in music, physical education, and art to help them represent ideas in many different ways. Each time teachers and administrators select these variables, they are expressing a hypothesis: if we devote more energy to this particular teaching strategy, then we should see a great improvement in student achievement.

The systematic application of holistic accountability helps teachers and school leaders in two important ways. First, it provides a research gold mine in which these hypotheses can be tested. For example, if we provide feedback that is timely and accurate, then— over many different students in different grades with different teachers—can we confirm the hypothesis that feedback is related to improved student performance? Second, it provides teachers with the opportunity to tell their professional story comprehensively and persuasively, even if their individual students are not among those who confirmed the hypothesis. These are teachers who, because of their students' high mobility and absenteeism, for example, do not show great improvements in test scores, but who nevertheless show great improvement in critical areas of teaching, curriculum, and leadership. These are teachers who might say, "We don't know if student scores improved, because the students moved twice during the year. But we can say definitively that the students who were here wrote more frequently, received more feedback, provided consistent evidence of reflection, analysis, and skill improvement, and engaged their parents in learning far more than their counterparts the year before." This approach to holistic accountability provides meaningful information for teachers and, of equal importance, seizes the initiative from the superficial emphasis on test scores that dominates media discussions of educational accountability.

Can we guarantee that newspapers will print the results based on teacher effort? Can we guarantee that talk-radio hosts will stop to consider a picture of educational accountability that is more complex than box scores? Certainly not. But we absolutely can guarantee that a more nuanced and comprehensive consideration of educational accountability will never happen if teachers and school leaders do not proactively share their stories and their data. If we do not promote holistic accountability, no one will do it for us.

Finally, even if the media never prints the results of the extraordinary work of teachers and leaders, even if improvements in curriculum remain invisible, these elements of progress are simply the right thing to do. Even if the only audience for holistic accountability consists of the teachers and leaders who embrace this technique, it remains valuable for every professional in the system and for all the children we serve.

3

The Accountable Teacher

The three schools profiled in this chapter will seem familiar to many readers. They are staffed by committed and hard-working teachers and administrators who are sometimes bewildered and even angry about the pressures under which they must work. These educators face competing demands for their time, including demands from students, parents, and colleagues whose needs of the moment can eclipse a consideration of long-term strategies. Stale cookies and strong coffee are standard fare, along with camaraderie and rivalry, support and isolation, satisfaction and frustration. These are, in brief, real schools. But each of these schools is remarkably different from the norm in a very specific way: they have managed to transform educational accountability from a destructive and demoralizing force into a constructive way to improve student achievement and professional satisfaction. Although the names and locations have been changed, the people and their stories are very real.

Walt Whitman Elementary School*

The teacher's lounge at Whitman Elementary seems at first glance to be comfortably familiar. Along one wall is a large couch with frayed upholstery, accompanied by unmatched furniture acquired or donated over the years. The distinctive smell of "teacher's coffee"—started hours ago and now being distilled to the consistency of maple syrup—is in the air. Cartoons poking gentle fun at life in school cover the refrigerator. But one distinctive feature in the Whitman lounge is startlingly different. A large bulletin board, eight feet wide and four feet tall, is covered with tables, charts, and graphs. In 12-inch lettering above the bulletin board are the words "Whitman Data Wall." A closer look reveals that the data wall contains much more than last year's test scores; it displays a rich variety of data, the vast majority of which were collected and analyzed by teachers on the Whitman faculty. This wall is the focal point of both formal faculty meetings and the innumerable informal discussions that happen in the faculty lounge. Teachers testify that it is these informal discussions that are the most helpful in improving their professional practices. Let's take a closer look at Whitman's data wall and listen to some of the conversations that it generates.

A Closer Look at the Data Wall

Charts and graphs in a school are not that unusual, although most data displays are confined to a notebook in the principal's office that is trotted out only for the benefit of visitors from the central office. But Whitman's data wall is more than a showpiece for visitors. Plain-language headings for each section of the bulletin board correspond to each of Whitman's themes: "Safe and Respectful Learning Environment," "Student Achievement," "Distinguished Teaching," and "Leadership by Example"; on the left-hand side of the bulletin board are the labels "Effects—What We Achieve" and "Causes—How We Achieve." The rest of the board contains graphs

---

* Unless otherwise noted, the schools and individuals discussed are composite representations of authentic cases. The names and locations are fictitious.

corresponding to each category. Some of the graphs are generated by computer, and others are created by hand. Some of the hand-made charts appear to be the work of students.

The Language of Discovery

Data displays can be a sensitive issue. After all, in a society known for turning every numerical display into an opportunity for rating, ranking, sorting, and humiliating, the display of data is an invitation to comparison, and comparison invariably means the pronounce-ment of winners and losers. But the conversation around data at Walt Whitman Elementary School is focused on discovery, not fear.

"Mary Anne!" It's Ernestine Gunzleman, a veteran of more than 32 years in the classroom, calling on Mary Anne Schneider, who is now a third-year teacher but who is also a former student of Mrs. Gunzleman's—a fact neither of them forgets.

"Yes, Mrs. G?"

"That chart says you had every one of your students proficient in geometric forms. Your IEP students were proficient in geometric forms! What are you doing down there? Tell me about it!"

Everybody knows that Mrs. Gunzleman can be a little rough around the edges, particularly when she wants to know something. But there is something striking about a veteran of her status asking a third-year teacher about techniques for improving student achieve-ment. This is a conversation that would never have begun without the data wall.

"Actually, I didn't do it at all," Ms. Schneider responds. "The year before last we had a terrible problem with this part of the state test, and I was feeling totally overwhelmed and a little embarrassed. I mean, how hard can it be to remember that a trapezoid isn't the same as an ellipse? But a lot of my kids didn't know their basic math facts, and I didn't want to lose time in my math block to work on geometric shapes."

"So," Mrs. Gunzleman persists, "what did you do?"

"I got help from Orlando Griego, the art teacher," Ms. Schneider explains. "We worked together to create art units that included everything my students were required to know—triangles, rectangles, squares, rectangular prisms, circles, ellipses, spheres—oh yeah, and the trapezoid, rhombus, and parallelogram. I think that's all of them. He used graph paper at first, to help students get the link between the units along a line and the square units in the shape. They were very creative and made some wonderful designs, but they had to be able to explain to Mr. Griego the building blocks of each design in terms of the basic geometric shapes. They also had to show him the relationship between the measurements around the edges—length, width, perimeter, circumference—and the measurements of area and volume. So you see, Orlando gets the credit for this, not me. We didn't know if it would be successful, so it was just a pilot project last year; but I think he plans to ask you and the other faculty members if it would be all right if he does this for all of our students."

Discussion Questions: Walt Whitman Elementary School Case Study

1. How would you characterize the actions of each of the professionals in this case study? Describe in rich detail the personal and professional traits that Mrs. Gunzleman, Ms. Schneider, and Mr. Griego exhibited.

2. What information was required to begin and sustain this dialog? What specific pieces of information did these educators have?

3. What role did school and central office administrators play in this innovation and in the dialog? What role might they play in the future?

4. How can the school and district accountability plan be structured in order to systematically share the results of this innovative collaboration?

Commentary: Walt Whitman Elementary School Case Study

The teachers at Walt Whitman don't ignore test scores. They know that tests are part of the educational and political landscape. But they are not obsessed with them either. If they had been focusing only on scores, the teachers might have been so busy looking at the numbers that they would have forgotten to ask about the story behind the numbers. Perhaps the key phrase in the entire case is Mrs. Gunzleman's query: "What are you doing down there? Tell me about it!" This faculty approaches the data wall with a spirit of discovery. They know that their colleagues—novices and veterans alike—have effective practices that are not recognized as having an impact on teaching and learning without the evidence that student-centered accountability provides. Their mutual task is to look at the data in new ways and to ask questions.

The administration of the school didn't have a grand plan for integrating mathematics into art instruction or a mandate from the central office for a certain number of minutes to be devoted to the rhombus and the ellipse. Indeed, other schools in the district would find such mandates laughably inappropriate, because their data suggest a need to focus on English vocabulary and math problem solving. By creating a framework for discovery rather than a list of mandates, the administration of Walt Whitman empowered teachers to use accountability in a constructive way. The administration was not passive—the data wall stimulates discussion, provokes inquiry, and approaches the sensitive issues of teacher comparison in a quest to find great practice.

Thompson Middle School

The first thing a visitor notices close to the entry of Thompson Middle School is the trophy case. It isn't the athletic and academic trophies that catch the visitor's attention, but the neatly arranged essays, lab reports, geography reports, musical compositions, and pieces of art that dominate the trophy case. Every person passing this display—whether a new 6th grader or a visiting grandparent, board member, or guest speaker—knows within seconds that this is a school that values and honors academic achievement. Beyond the trophy case is a gold-bordered "Wall of Fame" that extends the length of the first hallway. When exemplary student work is retired from the trophy case, the names are removed and the work is placed on the Wall of Fame, where it stays indefinitely.

"We don't intend to run out of wall space for a very long time," says principal Connie Skinner. When I ask why the Wall of Fame has no students' names, Ms. Skinner explains, "In the trophy case, we honor individual and team achievement. But on the Wall of Fame, we are making clear to every student in the school that kids in this neighborhood and in this school are expected to shine. Not just some kids—all kids. The Wall of Fame gives them models of what great performance looks like. We keep it up year after year because we want students to know from the very first day of school what our expectations are."

It wasn't always this way. For the past 10 years, the percentage of students on free or reduced lunch at Thompson Middle School has been steadily increasing, from 55 percent in the 1990s to well over 70 percent today. "That's probably an underestimate," explains Ms. Skinner. "Some kids won't use the free lunch card, and many parents won't help us on the paperwork. In the past, our expectations were low. We were good in a few sports, but whenever the suggestion was made that we improve academic achievement, we shrugged our shoulders and wondered what more we could do with kids who came to us chronically unprepared for middle school."

Of course, every school, even high-poverty schools, has a few academic superstars. They're the ones whose work is displayed in the trophy case and on the Wall of Fame, I think. A few kids who break the mold surely do not make for a high-performing school. As we turn the corner, we enter the "commons," where students gather for meetings, performances, and assemblies. Five hallways radiate from the commons, and each one has its own Wall of Fame. Each piece of work is superior, comparable to the work produced by students at the city's most elite public and private schools. The walls include elaborate science reports; sophisticated social studies reports integrating history, geography, and culture; and essays of every genre, including creative writing, poetry, research papers, and more. This is not the work of a few students.

Noticing my surprise, Ms. Skinner says, "We don't have 100 percent of our students represented on the Wall yet, but that's my goal. Every 6th grade student who enters this school should find at least one area where they can shine, where their work is truly exemplary. Some of the work you see went through seven or eight drafts. It was excruciating. But we knew that if we put poor work on the Wall of Fame, it would destroy everything we are trying to build. So it takes some kids longer and takes other kids multiple attempts, but I'm not going to rest until every student and every teacher has work represented on the Wall. So far, only 64 percent of our students have work that has qualified—we need to do a lot better than that."

So what do the teachers think? I wander into the door marked "Teachers Only," thinking it is the coffee room. I am in for a surprise. It is a mess. That isn't the surprising part. Rather, I am surprised by the contents of the mess. Every square inch of wall space is dominated by a series of bulletin boards with names on them: "Campbell," followed by "Anderson," then "Goldberg." This is middle school chaos, I remind myself, so I shouldn't expect alphabetical order. To make matters worse, the bulletin boards are not neat displays, but appear to be random sheets of paper—some computer-generated charts, some handmade graphs, and some paragraphs. Each board is festooned with haphazardly placed Post-It notes. Ruth Goldberg has just finished adding her own contribution to the mess when she turns to me and says, "I've been wondering about that."

"Wondering about what?" I ask.

"Why Stephanie Anderson is kicking butt in the scientific method," she says, without further elaboration. "That's my note." I look at the bulletin board labeled "Anderson" and, amid a flurry of other adhesive notes, find Ms. Goldberg's bold purple ink and capital letters asking, "HOW ARE YOU KICKING BUTT IN THE SCIENTIFIC METHOD???" The other notes I notice have one thing in common—they are all questions. On each bulletin board, every teacher at Thompson Middle School had posted success stories, supported by data, and every other teacher had left notes asking questions for clarification, questions about method, questions about curriculum, and questions about individual students. Another note says, "How did the inclusion kids do?" Another asks, "What did you give up to spend extra time on scientific method?"

As Ms. Goldberg walks out, Ms. Skinner comes in. "This is the agenda," she says.

"The agenda for what?"

"These notes—questions that colleagues ask one another about their best professional practices—form the agenda for everything we do—faculty meetings, grade-level meetings, team meetings, and professional development. If it isn't related to the questions our own professionals ask, then we don't spend time on it."

I ask how she can possibly know the answers to all of these questions. With a look normally reserved for a 7th grader who has just asked the most bizarre question, Ms. Skinner patiently explains, "*I don't.* I stopped running faculty meetings and staff development a long time ago. Besides, how can I teach chemistry to Ruth Goldberg? I'm English, she's science—I can't know every subject in a secondary school, so I don't try. But we work together to create this living agenda, and we have internal expertise for almost all of these questions. We might spend half a meeting on a question that influences all of us—something about classroom management or parent communication. Then we might spend the other half in huddles, with science teachers asking a colleague about recent gains in science scores, and music teachers offering ideas on how to improve student achievement on the fractions portions of the math tests. If we get stuck, we collectively take responsibility for finding external resources to help us. Almost all the time our faculty can provide a good response, and my job is to capture the questions and answers so that we can publish our book each year."

Which book does a group of middle school teachers publish? Ms. Skinner hands me a copy of last year's edition. The bold title is simple: *Best Practices in Teaching and Learning at Thompson Middle School, Volume III.* In small letters on the front cover are the authors—every teacher in the school who contributed at least one question and answer to the book. Ms. Skinner explains, "We use these as an end-of-year gift to every faculty member and as a welcome gift to every new faculty member. We know what works here, and we document it. When people from outside the school doubt that statement, we also give them the same gift as a gentle reminder that this is a place where accountability means the systematic identification and replication of best practices."

"But what about test scores?" I ask.

"Those are important," replies Ms. Skinner. "No doubt about it. But the scores don't help us understand the how and why of learning if we don't talk about professional practices. In fact, our scores have improved for four consecutive years. We now outscore schools that have only half the percentage of free and reduced lunch students that we have. But that would be an empty victory if we didn't understand how to replicate those practices and continue to improve."

"How do teachers feel about being so vulnerable and revealing their own test scores and individual professional practices?"

Before Ms. Skinner can answer, Ms. Goldberg is back. She answers as she walks by. "We hate it. Or at least we used to. Hey, we were getting hammered by the newspaper, by the board, by the public—our scores were out there anyway. At least now—in this room—we focus on our strengths, we ask questions, we get answers. It's like living in a laboratory. It's not always comfortable, but it beats the heck out of the old ways of annual scores, anger, and excuses. I'm not saying I like it yet—I told Connie it would never work. But I have learned a few things, and I think I've been able, for the first time in 20 years, to share things with my colleagues. That feels good. Connie even listens to my ideas. Look around you— there are a lot of smart teachers in this school, and we're getting smarter each time one of those Post-It notes goes up on the wall."

Discussion Questions: Thompson Middle School Case Study

1. Think of a time when you learned something from a colleague and a time when a colleague learned something from you. Describe those relationships and what happened to create a learning environment among adults. Describe the dynamics of the adult learning environment at Thompson Middle School. How is that similar to or different from your own learning experiences?

2. What was most surprising about the case study? Are there any ideas that the teachers and leaders at Thompson are using that you have never seen before? If all the ideas are familiar, are there any that you have never seen on such a large scale before?

3. What was the most expensive element of Thompson's improvement efforts? Are those expenses a barrier to replicating their ideas in your own school?

4. What were the emotional and psychological components of the Thompson ideas? Describe the emotional and psychological dynamics necessary for students and teachers to make the Thompson system remain effective.

Commentary: Thompson Middle School Case Study

Thompson Middle School exemplifies the learning organization. It's a safe place to ask questions and a rich place to find answers. It is far from a perfect place, with one-third of the students requiring intensive academic intervention and a growing number of students coming from a background of economic deprivation. It would be easy for teachers to retreat to their classrooms and do their best, knowing that the 18 hours of the day each student spends outside of school are far more influential on their achievement than the 6 hours they spend within the walls of Thompson. But thanks to teacher-created and teacher-led accountability, they must confront the power of their own impact on student achievement every day.

Middle schools are exhausting places, with students whose mood swings are bewildering and whose physical size can be intimidating. Middle schools can be exasperating places, as the eager 5th grade learner can become the taciturn and diffident 7th grade student. Middle schools can, like comprehensive high schools, be incredibly complex places, with a principal who is routinely overwhelmed with administrative and disciplinary duties and thus is rarely an instructional leader.

So what makes Thompson Middle School so vibrant? Is the faculty exceptionally enlightened? Ms. Goldberg's has been there two decades and knows that the difference between malaise and effectiveness is the collective will of the faculty to focus on their strengths, to ask one another questions, and to take responsibility for their professional growth and the achievement of their students. Does Thompson have exceptional resources? Their main investment appears to be in cardboard, tape, glitter, and Post-It notes—probably less than a fraction of the cost of many middle school reforms that have been launched and subsequently dissolved into oblivion. Is their principal exceptional? Perhaps only in her recognition that she cannot be the universal expert in every area and her understanding that no federal law requires that faculty meetings be convened by someone with an administrator's license. In fact, the most exciting part of Thompson Middle School is how ordinary the circumstances are and how extraordinary the results are. The only extraordinary thing the teachers do is to model the process of inquiry and learning on a daily basis, and that is something that every professional educator lives to do.

Richardson High School

"This place was originally built for 1,500 students," says Rita Akins, the perpetual motion machine who serves as the principal of this sprawling campus. "But nobody told that to parents 15 years ago, and now we've got more than 2,700 sets of walking hormones in our hallways and a faculty that has come very close to burnout and revolt. The highest of the high-stakes tests students will ever have take place in high school, and we're trying to teach way more than two years of academic content in the 9th and 10th grades. At the end of 10th grade, you see, they must take the state-mandated high school exit exam, and that requires mastery of material they have learned in elementary and middle school. Remove your hat, please, Mr. Sackett," Ms. Akins says in a pleasant but firm tone to a six-foot-four 11th grader with shoulder-length hair and innumerable facial piercings. "Oh, yes—the high school exit exam. They say that students can take it as many times as they want, but as a practical matter, the most persistent students will get five chances—the end of 10th grade, then twice in 11th grade and twice in 12th grade.

Most students are not that persistent. If we don't get them ready by the end of 10th grade, then there is a very significant chance that they will drop out. I lose sleep over the prospect of dropouts every night—we just can't lose these kids." Rounding the corner into her remarkably neat office, Ms. Akins breaks up a pair of students whose hearts are entwined and whose hands are invisible.

The "office" is actually a corner of the faculty lounge, with a small desk, a telephone, and every wall covered by bulletin boards and charts. "It's convenient," she explains. "Closer to the donuts." Her diet of chocolate-covered donuts and black coffee has taken no apparent toll on the slim Ms. Akins, who has yet to sit down at her desk. Motioning me to a chair, she explains, "Sorry. I never sit down. I'll just have to get up and go somewhere anyway." Her six-foot telephone cord allows her to wander around the room while talking on the phone, pacing and gesturing during each animated conversation. "The official principal's office is now a meeting room available for private conferences by any of the staff to meet with students, parents, or one another. I use it when I really need privacy, but 90 percent of the time my discussions can—and probably should—take place within earshot of any faculty member who happens to be around here. Besides, I enjoy their company."

The Richardson Data Center

With 2,700 students, Richardson High School might be expected to succumb to the obvious temptation to reduce student performance to averages and summaries. What is striking is how the faculty and leadership at Richardson have managed to maintain a focus on the needs of individual students. I ask about the bulletin board labeled "Opportunity Academy." An emphatic statement in large type states: NOBODY FALLS THROUGH THE CRACKS.

"The Opportunity Academy is the difference between success and dropping out for about 20 percent of our students," Ms. Akins explains. "I've got to run, but here's Otis Jackson—he'll explain it to you. Ask anybody around here about the other bulletin boards. Everybody knows what they mean and how we use them."

After the hasty departure of the principal, I introduce myself to Dr. Jackson, a meticulously attired man whose manner commands respect before he has said a single word. "The Opportunity Academy is the heart and soul of this school," he tells me. "These are the students who used to fail Algebra I three times and were our 18-year-old sophomores before anyone seemed to notice that we had a problem. Some of them learned to play the game, received *D*s, and were therefore totally invisible because they appeared to be successful. But we always knew that *D*s were just the coward's *F*s—failure that no one was willing to name. When I first came here, I found that 61 percent of students failing the high school exit examination had been routinely receiving *C*s and *D*s—good enough to get by, they thought. Now we know that these kids were sucker-punched. We told them that they were doing just fine, or at least good enough, and then we told them that they wouldn't be graduating after all. It was a disgrace. Now with the Opportunity Academy, we identify them immediately—in most cases before they enroll in 9th grade. If they are not identified for the Academy before enrollment, we identify them as in need of assistance within their first few weeks of school. Failures are not an option." Dr. Jackson's last statement is made with such determination that it is clear he is not repeating a slogan.

"Look at the bulletin board," he says. "You see the names of every student in the Academy, along with their current academic progress. We update this board every two weeks—nine-week report cards are way too late to provide meaningful feedback for these students. We want every faculty member in the school to know about these students, to see their potential, to celebrate their progress. I'm telling you, some of these students are going to be in honors classes two years from now. I love taking the Advanced Placement and honors teachers over to this board and showing them the names of students who are making tremendous progress and who, with some love, encouragement, and coaching, will be in their prestigious classes in the future."

The contents of the board are not very sophisticated. They certainly do not list every test, every standard, or every class. Rather, a few "Critical Indicators" are listed:

- Attendance Rate (Numbers lower than 90 percent are printed in red.)

- Reading Grade Level (Numbers lower than nine are printed in red.)

- Writing Level (This is scored on a rubric, ranging from Exemplary to Proficient to Progressing to Not Meeting Standards. Any level lower than Proficient is printed in red.)

- Study Skills (This is also scored on a rubric, with any level lower than Proficient printed in red.)

- Jazz (This column lists things such as football, ballet, cartoons, video games, classical music, and a host of other apparently unrelated activities.)

I have seen many data walls, but never any that mentioned video games or ballet. What is going on here? My perplexed look invites Dr. Jackson's explanation. "Jazz—that's the personal interest of each students. We need to know what gets them jazzed. I supposed it's an archaic expression to the kids and perhaps even to a few of my colleagues, but I chose it with a purpose. You see, jazz musicians never work alone. Part of what makes jazz is not just their individual interest and expertise, but how they cooperate with other players. Each student must find something that represents their personal jazz—the thing they love so much they do it not for money or for a grade, but because it's beautiful, engaging, and amazing. We use that spark of interest to the maximum extent possible to link our teaching strategies to their interests.

"Of course, we have lots of other data on these students, but we use this bulletin board to create an awareness of our critical indicators. If we have a student who is not proficient in reading and writing for their grade level, then I don't need a lot of statistics and test scores—I need to do whatever is necessary to help that student learn to read. We'll change schedules, arrange for tutoring, change study halls, and double or even triple class periods. I know that it sounds crazy and it sure is inconvenient, but we decided that it was a lot less inconvenient than seeing these students fail. It seems we always have time for remediation and actions after a failure, and now we invest that time, energy, and money to prevent failure. We look at this board during every single faculty meeting and ask how we can better meet the needs of these students. It's interesting that we get ideas not only from the Opportunity Academy faculty, but also from our colleagues who teach in other areas. We've had fantastic advice from special education, second-language educators, and teachers in our most advanced honors classes. The technology faculty has been incredibly helpful in brainstorming ways to reach disengaged and demoralized students. With 2,700 kids total and more than 500 in the Opportunity Academy, you might wonder how we accomplish this on a large scale. I guess the only answer I can give you is this—one student at a time. There's Robert—one of my stars. Got to go."

As Dr. Jackson leaves, I look around the room. The other bulletin boards represent the diversity one might expect of a comprehensive high school with many interests, divergent views, and multiple needs. One bulletin board is devoted to cartoons, including more than a few lambasting tests, administrators, legislators, and teachers.

"Can't take a joke?" Melissa Malone introduces herself, noticing that I am surprised that such contentious cartoons appear in a faculty lounge of a public high school. "They haven't repealed the First Amendment—yet," she explains. The chair of the social studies department, Dr. Malone has been an outspoken critic of standards and testing, yet here she is, adding another political cartoon to the board and updating the adjacent bulletin board with the title "Student Scholarship—Research and Publications." The board includes an astonishing array of student publications ranging from letters to the editor of the local newspaper to the *Concord Review,* a journal of the nation's best high school writing in history, to several online magazines.

"Sure, we keep track of test scores, including both the state tests and our own building-based assessments," Dr. Malone continues. "But in high school, it's not enough to settle for minimum competency or just getting by. We have to challenge these students to do work they never thought they could do, like getting national recognition through publication in competitive journals and Web sites. When they get e-mail from teachers, students and—my personal favorite—college admissions officers, they think of themselves in a far different way. You see our neighborhood and you've seen the kids—not a lot of designer clothes or new cars in the parking lot. These kids have never thought of themselves as scholars before. But the students who are on this board are scholars, and they know it. The world knows it. And I assure you that there will be more names on this board the next time you come here. Sorry, but I'm due in the library to coach a new teacher on our research protocols. Catch you later." And with that, Dr. Malone makes her exit.

Discussion Questions: Richardson High School Case Study

1. Think of educators and administrators you know who share the personal characteristics of the professionals in this case study. Identify some real-life examples of Dr. Malone, Ms. Akins, and Dr. Jackson.

2. Consider how your school deals with underachieving students. Think of both the timing and the content of the interventions that are typically used. How are those interventions similar to or different from the strategies employed at Richardson High School?

3. Consider just one idea that you noticed in the Richardson case study that is most appealing to you. Assuming that your school maintains its current level of resources in terms of time, money, and people, how could you implement that idea in your school?

4. Much of the data on the Richardson data walls would be invisible in the typical accountability report. How can the school and the district accountability plan be structured in order to systematically share the results of the innovative ideas employed at Richardson?

Commentary: Richardson High School Case Study

One of the accepted maxims of school reform discussions is that high schools are the last bastion of institutional resistance. Sure, the cynics say, one can change elementary schools—those people are enthusiastic about anything. But our high school faculty? Not a chance. They're cynical, recalcitrant, set in their ways, and have a thousand ways of undermining any reform. Besides, they've seen it all before and can outlast any superintendent or principal with new ideas. The interesting thing about Richardson High School is the distinct absence of "new ideas," unless one regards fundamental notions of academic excellence, human compassion, and a moral commitment to equity as inventions of the 21st century. As was the case in the first two case studies, the leadership was shared among administrators and teachers, with teachers taking a strong lead not only in the accountability for student learning but in the sharing of information with colleagues for the continuous improvement of instruction. It's tempting to call this school innovative, but the actual accountability mechanisms that they use are quite ordinary. Just a few subtle changes—visibility of information, accessibility of leadership, common commitment to excellence and equity, and the concomitant pursuit of excellence for the lowest- and highest-achieving students—are the factors that come together to make this school nothing short of remarkable. The danger in any description of remarkable schools, of course, is that the reader will sigh and exclaim, "Sure they could do it—but they were special. It could never happen at my school." But however special Richardson High School may be, it is not extraordinary and hardly unique.

A Note on Case Studies

To some people, the case study technique seems removed from reality. Does the case study format really have value? The endurance of the case study in the pages of the Harvard Business Review and the use of this technique in some of the nation's top schools of business, law, and medicine suggest that it is a powerful learning device for students who, to put it mildly, demand realism. In the context of education, case studies are particularly valuable. First, they force a discussion of specific behaviors of individual professionals. This rarely occurs in discussions of abstract theory that are too typical of many professional development seminars. Case studies also allow for a consideration of issues and behaviors in a depersonalized, and therefore less sensitive, environment than is the case when the discussion focuses on real people and situations in the school. Credible case studies retain the asset of realism while discarding the distractions of personalities and individual defensiveness. Finally, case studies allow professionals to synthesize their experiences from multiple contexts and bring to bear a rich variety of experiences in a compressed period of time.

In brief, the case study is a very useful technique for faculty meetings and professional development settings. Ideally, reactions to case studies include both those of individual professionals and those of groups working through the issues together. The divergent reactions to the same case provide for an illuminating exchange of ideas that, eventually, can be applied to the real issues facing your school.

4

Teacher Empowerment: Bottom-Up Accountability

Although I recoil at the imagery of teachers at the bottom of anything, including the hierarchy of the school system, there is no better term than "bottom-up accountability" to emphasize the clear contrast between an accountability system that empowers teachers and the prevailing "top-down" accountability system. In the prevailing model, teachers are the factory workers and students are the products to be manufactured to the exact specifications of the factory managers and owners. The quality of the product is measured principally by behavior and test scores. Good teachers have good test scores, the logic goes, and bad teachers have bad test scores. The field of "value-added" accountability (Sanders, 1998) relies upon this assumption.

Myth #1: Good Test Scores = Good Teaching

It is certainly true that teachers have a significant effect on student achievement as measured by test scores. It is also true that many other factors, including attendance, parental involvement, student motivation, and building-level leadership also have an effect. My graduate students in statistics learn perhaps only a couple of worthwhile lessons in my class, but they are important lessons. The first is "Life is multivariate." That is, every effect probably has multiple causes. This is surely the case when the effect to be examined is student achievement. The second lesson, particularly important for students of educational statistics to bear in mind, is "Not everything can be measured with a number."

It would be convenient and comfortable to stop the analysis with a consideration of test scores, but the teaching profession must come to grips with its own role in perpetuating the mythical association of high test scores and good teaching. Long-term patterns of teacher assignment play a significant role in this relationship, and the teaching profession—and those who represent teachers at the bargaining table—must acknowledge their role in resolving this challenge.

Teacher Assignment and Student Achievement

The logical flaw in the reasoning of most accountability systems is that some of the students who produce good test scores do so for reasons that have far more to do with the attributes of their family—income, language, and location—than the characteristics of the classroom teacher. The persistently noted correlation between good teachers and high test scores may, in fact, be a function of the traditional way in which teacher assignments are made. The least qualified and least experienced teachers are frequently assigned to the lowest-performing students in the lowest-performing schools. Professor Robert Ingersoll (2003) has documented this pattern throughout the United States. His studies are strongly supported by the observations of other researchers (Reeves, 2000a), who note the pervasive practice of using seniority, rather than equity, as the principal basis for teacher assignment.

In my individual interviews with educators defending this system, I have heard some veteran teachers refer to their ability to gravitate toward schools that have fewer poor and minority students as a "perk" that they have earned. Although perhaps these educators intend no racism or economic discrimination, the unmistakable impression is that educators' advancement, skill, higher status, and experience in their system are associated with the reward of being in contact with students who are economically advantaged and who share an Anglo heritage, whereas inexperience, lower status, inferior skill, and subordination characterize teachers who are routinely in contact with students who are economically disadvantaged and who are ethnic minorities.

This is not always the case, and one can find exceptions in which veteran teachers with advanced degrees are routinely assigned to the lowest-performing students in the most challenging schools. In addition, there are wonderful examples of teachers who continually volunteer for the most difficult teaching assignments. But these cases, however noteworthy, are exceptional. The far more common assignment pattern has the most experienced and qualified teachers migrating away from students who most need them. Thus, if we are to counter the prevailing attitude that "good test scores = good teaching," then the teaching profession must address the manner in which teachers are assigned to schools.

How can the traditional cycle of teacher assignment be broken? Arbitrary reassignment is unlikely to be effective. When Chancellor Harold Levy, former leader of the New York City Public Schools, attempted to transfer teachers from low-poverty to high-poverty schools, he was inundated with resignations. If the arbitrary imposition of authority is ineffective, how about financial incentives? Ingersoll and Smith (2003) found that while low pay was a concern for many teachers leaving high-poverty schools, more departing teachers listed issues such as student discipline, poor administrative support, poor student motivation, and a lack of faculty influence. In other words, teachers demand a combination of economic and noneconomic considerations, including safety, time, and respect. Thus the ultimate resolution of the challenge of equitable teacher assignment does not depend merely on teacher bargaining units giving up their rights in assignment policies, but rather depends upon a combination of positive incentives so that experienced and highly qualified educators choose to serve our most challenging students. These incentives might include lower class sizes, additional planning time, greater administrative support, and unequivocal assurances of personal safety. As Ingersoll and Smith concluded, "these data suggest that the roots of the teacher shortage largely reside in the working conditions within schools and districts" (p. 32).

Myth #2: Bad Teaching Yields Good Test Scores

Some of the most noteworthy critics of school testing formulate the reverse of the "good test scores = good teaching" formula. The critics complain that the only path toward student achievement, as measured by traditional test scores, is mindless test drills. In such an environment, the critics contend, one does not have time to be a good teacher. If an educator were to devote time to creative endeavors, student engagement, critical thinking, and advanced writing, then these trivial pursuits would rob time from the frantic content coverage and test drills that are necessary for good test performance. By such logic, good teachers have bad test scores.

If these allegations are true, then classes characterized by creativity, engagement, and rigor—particularly those populated by economically disadvantaged students—should have low test scores. The data, however, do not support this hypothesis. In repeated observations across the country (Reeves, 2000b), I have found that the "diversion" of teacher time into having students write, edit, rewrite, and collaboratively score their work—even when these teaching choices come at the expense of frantic content coverage and test drills—are associated with higher, not lower, scores on state-mandated tests.

Thus both of the prevailing arguments in the testing debate are wrong. The proponents of high-stakes testing are wrong when they presume that they can evaluate teaching effectiveness solely on the basis of test scores. The critics of high-stakes testing are wrong when they presume that the pursuit of improved student achievement as measured by those test scores leads teachers to become mindless sycophants who forget everything they ever learned about critical thinking and student engagement. The resolution to this dilemma lies in the reformulation of educational accountability.

Teacher Leadership in Accountability

There is a constructive alternative to top-down accountability systems and the exclusive reliance on test scores. To validate effective teaching practices and at the same time recognize the need to measure student achievement, we can use a mix of educational variables and analytical methods. This holistic approach to educational accountability is comprehensive, fair, and constructive. A comprehensive approach to accountability includes not only a focus on *effect* variables, such as test scores, but also a deep understanding of *cause* variables. If teachers wish to transform accountability from a set of policies "done to" teachers and students to a constructive influence on teaching and learning, then teachers must take the lead in the systematic documentation of their practices in teaching and curriculum, and the relationship of those practices to student achievement. A growing number of teachers who have pursued certification through the National Board for Professional Teaching Standards (NBPTS) have already made such systematic observation and reflection a regular part of their professional practice (Darling-Hammond & Sykes, 1999). Educational accountability policies will fail to reach their potential, however, unless this sort of reflection becomes the norm rather than the exception.

Teacher leadership in accountability includes the following elements: (1) observation, (2) reflection, (3) synthesis, and (4) replication. Each of these elements is essential, and a holistic accountability system is incomplete without all four.

Observation

Accountable teachers know the extent to which their intended practice matches their actual performance. They know, for example, how often students can resubmit work based on timely teacher feedback. Accountable teachers know how often they collaboratively score student work, and they know the degree to which their assessment of student work is consistent with their colleagues' judgments. These educators know how often they have provided multiple contexts to reinforce the same intellectual idea—finding opportunities for compare-and-contrast writing in an art class, for social studies lessons in a music class, for measurement lessons in a physical education class, and for poetry lessons in a science class. They know that students this year have received more frequent feedback than was the case last year, and they know that students have been challenged to think, analyze, reason, and write more frequently than last semester. The moments when these pedagogical advances happen are neither accidental nor serendipitous, but are the deliberate result of careful professional practice. These teachers know the hallmarks of effective practice and deliberately incorporate these techniques into every day. Moreover, they systematically observe their implementation of these techniques with a clear objective of providing a higher degree of effective practice this month than the previous month.

In watching a number of accountable teachers, I have been struck by the "low-tech" nature of their observation. They do not equate sophisticated observation of professional practice with elaborate displays. Some keep pencil-and-paper notes, and others maintain simple graphs. Some use computer spreadsheets, and others have their students construct graphs of various aspects of teacher performance, such as the frequency of feedback, making the students a partner in the creation of effective teaching and learning processes. Some display their tables, charts, and graphs for the world to see, and others reserve their sharing of professional practices for conversations with a colleague or a mentor. The first common theme of effective accountability is not showy displays, but quiet, consistent, and systematic observation.

The practice of systematic observation harbors a potential danger: the teachers who engage in this practice most seriously tend to be too hard on themselves. They are acutely aware when an underperforming student has gone for an entire week without personal and meaningful teacher feedback. Their own evidence convicts them when a busy month has passed in which little or no meaningful collaboration took place with a colleague.

The difference between these remarkable educators and their less effective colleagues is that the accountable educators are aware of their shortcomings and the need to make midcourse corrections, whereas the vast majority of people are lost in the busyness of the day and fail to recognize the need to make necessary adjustments until the school year is complete. The tendency of accountable teachers to drive themselves hard and to become dominated by critical voices is a central challenge for colleagues, mentors, and school administrators. Teachers who engage in systematic observation deserve encouragement, nurturing, and accolades, even when their observations frankly acknowledge some shortcomings. Researchers are guided by the maxim that "we learn more from error than from uncertainty." Similarly, the accountable teacher who confesses the need to improve professional practices after engaging in systematic observation deserves reinforcement and encouragement, not reproof.

Reflection

The second characteristic of the accountable teacher is reflection. The gathering of information on professional practice is of little value unless it includes regular reflection based on these questions:

- What worked?
- What do I notice about the relationship between these practices and student achievement?
- How were my most recent professional practices different from those of six months ago?
- When did I make the most meaningful connection with students? What precisely was I doing when those connections occurred?
- How are my observations consistent or inconsistent with those of my colleagues?

Reflection, therefore, requires not only the analytical task of reviewing one's own observations but also the more challenging task of listening to colleagues and comparing notes. The reflective process is at the very heart of accountability. It is through reflection that we distinguish between the popularity of teaching techniques and their effectiveness. The question is not "Did I like it?" but rather "Was it effective?" In my own classroom experiences with children as well as adults, I have been forced to confront more than once the difference between what I enjoyed (the sound of my own voice resonating with sophisticated language) and what my students most valued (my silent attention as I listened to them express complex ideas in their own words).

Reflection is an inherently collaborative activity, requiring the active participation of students and colleagues as co-conspirators in the relentless effort to improve teaching and learning. This approach to accountability transforms the role of student from "product" to colleague. It transforms the role of teacher from "factory worker" to research analyst, coach, and mentor. It is, in brief, an extraordinary amount of work and is a key to the transformation of accountability from a menial exercise in tallying test scores to an analysis of professional practices that offers insight and continuous improvement.

Synthesis

Case studies are the Rodney Dangerfields of educational research, garnering less respect than the pathetically needy comic. The contemporary emphasis on scientifically controlled study has diminished the credibility of case studies, rendering individual experience, in the judgment of critics, too trivial for serious consideration. Nevertheless, a strong case can be made for the value of case studies and other forms of qualitative research. The most important characteristic of good qualitative research is its rich description, a property that is absent in a recitation of quantitative measurements. Moreover, the accumulation of systematic observations allows for insights that are subject to quantitative analysis. A single case study may be an anecdote; a thousand case studies, by contrast, offer the potential for the creation of a body of evidence supported by quantitative analysis. The genesis of theories in biology, pharmacology, psychiatry, and education, to name just a few disciplines, emerges from the synthesis of many different case studies.

Synthesis is the hallmark of accountability research. In my reviews of accountability data from hundreds of schools (Reeves, 2000a, 2001a), the individual observations would never rise to the level of persuasive research. But when, for example, I note that all schools with gains of more than 20 percent in student achievement also happen to employ common assessments, extensive nonfiction writing, and collaborative scoring by the faculty, then I can begin to draw inferences that common assessments, nonfiction writing, and collaborative scoring are at the very least associated with improved student performance. These observations fall far short of any assertion of causation. The same was true of the initial observations of the coincidence of smoking and lung cancer, as tobacco company scientists gravely reminded the public in the 1960s. Nevertheless, the synthesis of hundreds and thousands of case studies allows researchers to eventually formulate theories and hypotheses that can be further subjected to rigorous inquiry.

In sum, although the systematic observations of teachers may not answer the questions of researchers, the combination of systematic observation and careful synthesis paves the way for further research. More important, the combination of observation and synthesis creates a constructive role for educational accountability, replacing prejudgment with fact and personal preferences with tested professional practices.

Replication

The final test of teacher leadership in accountability is not merely the rigor of the observations nor the sophistication of analytical synthesis, but rather our commitment to replicate effective practices. When presented with a new accountability system, teachers rightly ask, "What's in it for me?" Will this new accountability system, they wonder, really save time, improve achievement, and focus professional practice where it is most effective? The answer to those challenges is a resounding "no," unless the replication of effective practice is an integral part of accountability. Perhaps the most blunt and meaningful question one can ask of any research procedures is "So what?" In other words, "Now that we know that there is a higher likelihood of Y if we do X, are we really going to do X or just talk about it?" That is the fundamental question posed by teacher-led accountability. The leap from synthesis to replication forces educators and school leaders to confront questions such as the following:

- We know that writing, thinking, analysis, and reasoning are effective. Will we do more of it?

- We know that collaborative scoring of student work is associated with higher levels of fairness and greater levels of student performance. Will we expand it?

- We know that flexible schedules and greater investments of time in basic sources are associated with lower failure rates. Will we modify our schedules accordingly?

- We know that more frequent feedback is associated with improved student work ethic, motivation, and performance. Will we change the timing of our feedback?

In brief, the challenge of replication is at the heart of effective accountability. Without replication, accountability is a sterile exercise in reporting and evaluation. With all four of the essential characteristics of teacher-led accountability—observation, reflection, synthesis, and replication—we can transform accountability into a constructive force for students and society.

5

A View from the District

Accountability for learning is an empowering and exciting part of education. Traditional accountability systems limit teachers to the use of scores based on external indicators that may or may not be related to actual teacher performance. This inevitably leads to a sense of futility and hopelessness, robbing teachers and principals of the intrinsic motivation that was most likely the impetus for their decision to become educators in the first place. Accountability for learning, in contrast, enhances intrinsic motivation by commingling a sense of meaningfulness—the hallmark of intrinsic motivation—with a sense of competence and progress, the keys to maintaining that motivation (Thomas, 2002).

Consider the psychological dissonance that is inevitable when teachers see a sparkle in students' eyes, receive reinforcement from parents, and observe fine work in the classroom, and simultaneously are told that they are in a school labeled a failure because of the test scores of students who were not in the teacher's class, whose attendance was sporadic, and whose home environment did not support educational priorities. These teachers likely doubt the other feedback that they receive, ultimately regarding themselves as personal and professional failures. Once they give up hope, perception becomes reality, as their formerly heroic efforts give way to passivity. Their relentless optimism is overtaken by a sense of helplessness, with the former "You can do it!" replaced by "Nothing I do will make a difference."

If we stop the analysis here—as many commentators on accountability and assessment have done—the picture is bleak indeed, with the intrinsic motivation of teachers consigned to the ash pit of history. It does not have to be this way. A number of school systems have seized the opportunity to transform their accountability systems, to recognize teachers as integral parts of constructive accountability, and to use their systems to provide positive and meaningful feedback throughout the year for teachers, students, and administrators. These districts have the same political constraints, financial limits, union agreements, and human frailties as their counterparts throughout the world. But they have nevertheless taken advantage of the opportunity to make "accountability" a word that allows teachers to showcase their professionalism rather than cringe in horror.

The Imperatives of System-Level Leadership

The demands on superintendents and other system-level leaders are extraordinary and almost comically unreasonable. The literature on leadership adds little rationality to the discussion, expecting leaders to be some mythical combination of, in alphabetical order, Attila the Hun, Catherine the Great, Churchill, Elizabeth I, Jefferson, Jesus, Machiavelli, Moses, Napoleon, Nixon, Rasputin, Roosevelt (Teddy and Franklin), Washington, and untold numbers of yet to be reconstructed historical leaders whose biographers have found some link between personal traits and organizational effectiveness. I would like to offer more modest ambitions for leaders of complex educational systems.

Catch Teachers Doing Something Right

First, leaders must catch teachers doing something right. This is not obvious, because the traditional relationship between teachers and the central office is focused on compliance and enforcement. Finding errors, omissions, malfeasance, and misfeasance is the rule, not the exception. Little wonder, then, that teacher evaluation has devolved from an attempt to improve professional performance into a negotiated bureaucratic drill in which the interactions between teachers, principals, and other evaluators are limited in quantity and eviscerated in quality. Recent well-intentioned efforts, from walk-throughs to informal observations, offer some promise, but in practice these actions tend to be unsystematic and inconsistent, leaving teachers aware that leaders are more visible but without a clearer idea of expectations. Unfortunately, many of these informal observations focus on documentation—the posting of standards, the existence of a lesson plan, and the adherence to a schedule—rather than on professional practices that lead to student engagement and reflective practice.

It does not have to be this way. Exemplary leaders make it their mission to catch teachers doing something right. They create annual documents titled "Best Practices in Oak Trail Middle School" or "Exemplary Teaching in Pierce County School District." These documents bear the names of the contributing teachers on the cover and contain modest contributions, typically a single page and perhaps a picture for each professional practice. The practices described in these documents are exceptionally specific, such as the impact of a new lesson plan (Stevenson & Stigler, 1992) or a method of feedback that yields improved student achievement (Marzano, Pickering, & Pollock, 2001). The best practices captured in these documents are not limited to classroom interactions but also include specific strategies for engaging parents and community members (Reeves, 2002b).

Provide Focus

Second, leaders of educational systems must provide focus. The acid test of this book or any resource that purports to improve educational achievement must be that it inspires the reader to create a "not to do" list (Collins, 2001) rather than to pile one more initiative on the backs of teachers and school leaders. The "law of initiative fatigue" (Reeves, 2002b) is irrefutable: each additional initiative, program, task, or swell idea results in fewer minutes of time, fewer dollars, and generally less leadership attention and emotional energy of teachers to make each successive initiative work. For many years leaders have espoused the virtues of focus, even as they develop strategic plans that are more closely linked to deforestation than to improved student achievement.

Many school systems provide extraordinary examples of the principle of focus. The Norfolk Public School system in Virginia, for example, has only one board goal (Simpson, 2003). This stands in stark contrast to school systems that appear to equate quality with girth in their school and district plans. The Freeport, Illinois, schools have made stunning advances in both educational achievement and in equity despite school and district plans that are remarkably brief. In Wayne Township in Indianapolis, a myopic focus on accountability for learning has been associated not only with dramatically improved student achievement in a complex urban environment, but also with stunning gains in equity for poor and minority students.

As a guide to improved focus, school system leaders may wish to consider the "law of six" (Reeves, 2000a; 2002b), which states that neither leaders nor organizations can focus successfully on more than six goals. This applies whether we are considering the number of "top priority" tasks for an individual in a single day or the number of measurable indicators that a school purports to have in its school improvement plan. A cardinal principle of measurement states that it is more effective and accurate to measure a few things frequently rather than many things once a year.

Focus begins with the board of education and the superintendent, people who often are far more successful at creating new initiatives than at terminating old ones. To test the application of this principle in your own district, divide a piece of paper into two columns. Label the left-hand column with the heading "Initiatives Begun in the Last Five Years," and underneath the heading list the initiatives your district has undertaken in that time period. Label the right-hand column with the heading "Initiatives That Have Been Deliberately Reviewed and Terminated," and write a corresponding list below that heading. In almost all districts, the left-hand column is significantly longer than the right-hand column. Unless the dollars in your budget and the minutes in your day have expanded as much as the growth in your list of initiatives, you are certain to become a victim of initiative fatigue

Redefine Strategic Planning

The third obligation of system-level leaders is to redefine strategic planning. Elsewhere I have argued that we must "save strategic planning from strategic plans" (Reeves, 2002b). In too many instances, strategic plans have become a singularity, with the plan itself becoming the objective rather than the results the plan was to have achieved. System leaders must redefine strategic planning as a continuous process of leadership decisions based on information related to student achievement. The idea that a strategic plan should be "updated" once every five years assumes a stasis that is fundamentally inaccurate. Moreover, the disbanding of the strategic planning committees and task forces when "The Plan" is published makes clear that the document is elevated in public view and administrative attention over the hapless schleps who must execute the plan. A sad legacy of the "leadership/management" dichotomy of the past few decades is the haughty presumption that leaders think great thoughts, develop grand visions, and create thick plans, whereas mere managers (read "building principals and teachers") are the ones who bring those visions and plans to reality. In fact, leaders must be willing to get their hands dirty, sitting on the floor with kindergarteners, substituting for the absent chemistry teacher, standing next to the crossing guard, walking the hallways during passing period, and taking hot coffee to the bus drivers in the morning.

The requirement to redefine strategic planning does not imply that strategic planning should be abandoned or that the concept is unimportant. Rather, this is a plea that strategic plans become not merely the accumulation of what everyone on a community task force believes to be important. The most effective strategic plans are not those that are more impressive in their weight than their substance. If your school system already has a strategic plan, ask how you can make it shorter. If your school system has never had a strategic plan, ask whether the funds devoted to a plan generated by outsiders can be better spent executing a few well-chosen objectives developed by insiders.

Create Holistic Accountability

The fourth imperative for system-level leadership is the creation of holistic accountability (Reeves, 2001a). The premise of holistic accountability is that educational accountability is more than test scores. Although test scores have long been an important part of the educational and political landscape, an exclusive emphasis on test scores as the primary indicator of educational quality is based on a false analogy to the business world, in which "results" are sometimes regarded as the only measure of achievement. During the booming stock market of the 1990s, such an analogy was frequently praised, with the results in business (stock prices and reported earnings) masquerading as sufficient indicators of quality. All that mattered was the bottom line, and factors such as deteriorating employment base, restatements of earnings, and accounting irregularities were minor inconveniences as long as stock prices and reported earnings soared. Then came Enron and a host of lesser-known corporate debacles, which wiped out more than a trillion dollars of shareholder value. Readers of this volume who hardly paid attention to the stock market in the past watched in disbelief as the value of retirement plans sank, college savings plans evaporated, and the personal consequences of corporate malfeasance spread from the boardroom to the family room. As the disaster unraveled, it became clear that the proverbial bottom line had been an illusion. The focus on corporate results had diverted attention from warning signs that were, in retrospect, abundant and clear.

Every policymaker owes a debt of gratitude to Enron and its aftermath, because we now understand that an exclusive emphasis on test scores in educational accountability invites the inevitable spectacle of the "Educational Enron," in which an institution (a school, a district, or an entire state) that had gained public confidence through its rising test scores will come crashing down. Perhaps it will be the educational version of accounting irregularities, but the crash will more likely be due to behavior that is less malicious than it is rational.

Rational behavior, in the Skinner model of behavioralism, will seek reward and avoid punishment. Thus certain behaviors that improve test scores will be overlooked as surely as the profligacy of executives of companies whose soaring stock prices obscured the fact that their gains were illusory. Among the factors that will almost certainly lead to higher test scores are the following:

- Higher dropout rate, particularly among poor and minority students.

- Classification of higher numbers of students as special education students, legally entitled to alternative assessments or exclusion from assessments. (State attempts to limit test exclusions will be challenged, successfully, by a growing number of attorneys whose specialty is litigating with school districts who follow state testing guidelines rather than federal requirements for students' disabilities.)

- Reduction in the number of classes outside the core curriculum, including world languages, music, art, physical education, and technology, to name a few.

- Cross-district recruiting of potentially high-scoring students, using Internet-based classes, less restrictive attendance requirements, or other "affirmative action" policies that benefit students who represent ethnic and linguistic majorities, who are economically advantaged, and whose educational opportunities outside of school predispose them to higher test scores.

- Strategic warehousing of low-scoring students, thereby isolating any state or federal designation of "low-performing school" to a small number of predictable "problem" schools. These strategies will be supported by zero-tolerance policies of discipline in which infractions by low-scoring students will lead to their transfer out of schools.

- Lowering the definition of "meeting standards" so that rigor is replaced with sloth and competence is supplanted by test performance that is only somewhat better than random error. In other words, student performance will become less important than the labeling of that performance, often on a retrospective basis. In the greatest irony of all, the national push toward standards will be replaced by a retreat to the bell curve as lower averages lead to fewer challenges, which, in turn, lead to lower averages, followed by lower expectations. The diminution of performance will be irrelevant, however, because the performance labels respond to the public demand for higher percentages of students who are "proficient."

I hope that I am wrong and that two or three years after this book is published readers will mock my pessimism. But because examples of these phenomena already exist, it is at least equally likely that this list of stratagems will, in retrospect, appear too brief.

Just as observers have an alternative to the silly reductionism that equated corporate success with ephemeral short-term earnings and stock prices, educators and others have a better way to view educational accountability. Holistic accountability is such an alternative. Just as effective corporate accountability considers the factors underlying earnings, holistic accountability considers the antecedents of educational excellence, including the following factors:

- Teaching practices, including assessment, feedback, and collaboration, to name a few.

- Curriculum practices, including equity of opportunity for enrollment in advanced classes.

- Leadership practices, including the use of resources to support the most important educational priorities. At its best, holistic accountability includes not merely measurements of what teachers and administrators do, but also a consideration of the actions of board members and other policymakers (Simpson, 2003).

- Parent involvement, including not only participation in school volunteer activities, but also substantive activities at home and in the community.

- Faculty communication, including intergrade and interdepartment collaboration.

- Professional development, including study of research, pedagogy, assessment, and content area.

In other publications I have elaborated on the variables that can be examined as part of holistic accountability (Reeves, 2000a; 2001a; 2002b; 2002d). Suffice it to say that effective school systems know the difference between effects and causes, between test scores and the antecedents of excellence.

Accountability for Learning: A Case Study of Effective Practice

The Norfolk Public School system is a complex urban system with more than 34,000 students, of whom 67 percent are members of racial minorities. Virginia was one of the first states to adopt rigorous academic standards and detailed testing requirements, and the first test results in the 1990s were miserable. The poor urban districts (or school divisions, as they are called in Virginia) in particular suffered terrible public ridicule based on the initial test results. Many test critics regarded the low test scores as clear evidence that the standards were impossible to meet and must be inherently biased against children in environments characterized by high percentages of poor and minority families. Although surely the intent of those critics was not racism, their message was clear: those kids just can't do it. The underlying theory of ethnic and economic determinism was inescapable. Fortunately, teachers and administrators in Norfolk did not believe it. The results in this dynamic district, as presented by Superintendent John O. Simpson, speak for themselves:

> Like the city, Norfolk Public Schools, the first public school system in Virginia, has seen its fortunes go up and down. It is an urban district that serves a diverse population: 67 percent of students are black and 28 percent are white. More than 65 percent of students qualify for free and reduced-price lunches. . . .

- 100 percent of our schools met the state benchmarks in writing in all grades tested.

- 100 percent of our high schools met the state benchmarks in chemistry.

- 100 percent of our middle schools are fully accredited in earth science.

- 100 percent of our middle and high schools showed positive trends in reading, literature, and research.

Also, our schools reduced the achievement gap between white and black students in third, fifth, and eighth grades, with both groups continuing to improve. They decreased disciplinary actions by 15 percent, the number of long-term suspensions by 14 percent, and the number of expulsions by 66 percent.

In addition, we have two "90/90/90 schools." These are schools with more than 90 percent of students eligible for free and reduced-price lunch, more than 90 percent are minority students, and more than 90 percent of students met high academic standards on the state's Standards of Learning tests. (Simpson, 2003, pp. 43–44)

Going Beyond Test Scores

The moral principle at work in Norfolk is that no child in the system will be any more accountable than the adults. Thus it is no surprise that the first step in developing the accountability system was the establishment of accountability indicators for the board of education and a related commitment to publicizing those indicators as frequently as academic accountability indicators are reported for students (Reeves, 2002d). In addition, every central office department, from transportation to academic affairs, from food service to assessment, from recreation to finance, has accountability indicators that are reported along with student test scores. Indeed, each central office department and each board member are regularly challenged to identify the extent to which their decisions and leadership actions are related to the needs of students and teachers.

Each school building in Virginia must report its test scores—that is a matter of state law. But in Norfolk and other school systems with constructive accountability systems, each school also reports on several building-based indicators that are a direct reflection of teaching behaviors, leadership decisions, and curriculum policies. These building documents are publicly available, so that building principals and teachers can learn from one another, examining the best practices of their colleagues. They can identify those buildings and classrooms with significant gains in academic achievement and ask, "What are they doing that is different?" and "How are their professional practices related to improvements in student achievement?"

At the beginning of the 2002–03 school year, I examined the reports of each of the schools in Norfolk and asked those same questions. In particular, I wondered if the buildings that experienced gains of 20 percent or more in their academic achievement in language arts, mathematics, science, and social studies were significantly different from other schools in the system. The schools with the greatest gains were not similar demographically; they included high-poverty and low-poverty student populations. The financial support, staffing patterns, union agreements, and central office support were similar for all schools. Therefore, neither the demographic variables of students nor the external variables of funding and labor agreements could explain the extraordinary differences between the schools. The keys to improved academic achievement were the professional practices of teachers and leaders, not the economic, ethnic, or linguistic characteristics of the students.

Although surely effective organizations of all types share many other traits, the Norfolk accountability system provided an insight into measurable indicators that were linked to the largest gains in student achievement. These characteristics also make clear that successful accountability is not the exclusive domain of the "Department of Accountability" in the central office, but rather is a responsibility shared throughout the system on many levels. The examination of the Norfolk accountability system revealed striking similarities to other research on the characteristics of successful schools, including observations I have made in other school systems over the course of several years. The following paragraphs highlight the nine characteristics that distinguished the schools with the greatest academic gains.

The Impact of Collaboration. First, the schools provided time for teacher collaboration. This was not merely an exercise in idle discussion or an attempt to get along in a friendly and collegial fashion. Rather, meaningful collaboration meetings required an examination of student work and a collective determination of what the word "proficiency" really means. At first, teachers were alarmed to see how the same piece of student work received strikingly different evaluations from different teachers. In the course of many sessions—the most effective schools made time for collaboration very frequently and in some cases did this every day—teachers narrowed their differences by agreeing on certain characteristics of acceptable student work.

Where did schools find the time for effective collaboration? None of these schools had extra money in the budget or more hours in the day. Rather, they used the time that they already had with an intentional focus on collaborative scoring of student work. For example, the principals made their faculty meetings "announcement-free zones." Rather than drone through a laundry list of announcements during faculty meetings (with inevitable comments and controversies), they decided that the transmission of information would always be in writing. This allowed time formerly used for announcements to be dedicated to collaboration. The principals were literally on the same side of the table as their faculty members, with teachers who were experienced in collaborative scoring taking turns facilitating faculty meetings. The other source of time for collaboration was professional development meetings. Rather than presentations by outside staff developers, a significant amount of the professional development time was allocated to collaborative scoring. These educators knew that collaboration is hard work. Moreover, they understood that it is a skill acquired over time. Hence these remarkably effective schools did not have a "collaboration day" or a "collaboration workshop" but rather made the collaborative scoring of student work a part of their regular routine.

The Value of Feedback. Second, the schools with significant improvements provided much more frequent feedback to students than a report card typically provides. Emulating their most successful colleagues in music and physical education, teachers provided feedback in real time. They knew that a basketball coach does not provide hints on an effective jump shot nine weeks after a flubbed attempt, nor does a great music teacher mention the improper position of a violinist's left hand weeks after noticing the mistake; but rather coaches and musicians provide precise and immediate feedback. In some cases, teachers took a triage approach, providing successful and self-directed students with traditional report cards and providing struggling students with weekly progress reports. Their approach to feedback was consistent with the findings of Robert Marzano and his colleagues, whose meta-analysis of research revealed that feedback had a profound impact on student achievement, provided that the feedback was timely, accurate, and specific (Marzano, Pickering, & Pollock, 2001). The emphasis that these teachers placed on accuracy in feedback was remarkable. Unlike the "positive distortion" that clouds so much classroom feedback (Foersterling & Morgenstern, 2002), the feedback provided by teachers whose students made large gains was consistently accurate, with student performance compared to unambiguous expectations.

The Impact of Time. Third, the schools with large gains made dramatic changes in their schedule, despite having the same budget, state requirements, teachers union contract, and other restrictions as other schools in the system. At the elementary level, they routinely devoted three hours each day to literacy, with two hours of reading and one hour of writing. At the secondary level, they routinely provided double periods of English and mathematics. This was not a shell game in which they used the block schedule to double up on English and math some times but cut back at other times. Rather, it represented a genuine increase in instructional hours of math and English. The essential importance of instructional time is hardly a new idea, yet in an astonishing number of schools, the schedule is revered more than the Pledge of Allegiance, the Constitution, and the Magna Carta combined. To break the mold in student achievement, these schools discovered, they had to break the schedule. It is interesting that this commitment to time for literacy instruction occurred in a state that required examinations in social studies and science. These teachers and principals did not change the schedule because they wanted to emphasize literacy at the expense of science and social studies, but rather because they knew that literacy was essential for success in every content area.

Action Research and Midcourse Corrections. Fourth, teachers engaged in successful action research and midcourse corrections. In many of the schools with the greatest gains, accountability plans were not static documents set in concrete before the beginning of the school year, but dynamic and flexible guides. These schools asked the central office for permission to change goals and strategies that were not effective and to start new ones that held promise, even during the school year. Moreover, these faculties and leaders learned from one another. An illustration of their commitment to the application of action research is the use of "word walls" at the secondary level. Because both the school improvement data and the instructional techniques associated with those improvements are transparent in a holistic accountability system, the teachers who had achieved great things with students were subject to questions from colleagues throughout the system about their success. After elementary educators reported that significant improvements in vocabulary and reading comprehension results were associated with the implementation of word walls, the secondary science and social studies teachers decided to adopt the idea. They created walls covered with essential science and social studies vocabulary words, sometimes adding vivid visual images, and they used those vocabulary words throughout the year. In other examples of effective action research, teachers replicated one another's writing rubrics, interdisciplinary assessments, and student motivation practices.

Aligning Teacher Assignments with Teacher Preparation. Fifth, principals made decisive moves in teacher assignments. Some writers have argued that when test scores are down, the entire school should be reconstituted and the entire faculty dismissed. In my observations, however, I have seen principals make impressive gains by reassigning teachers to different grades within the same school. Consider what has happened to the curriculum—particularly in the 4th, 5th, and 6th grades—over the past decade. The complexity of the curriculum has increased enormously, particularly in math and science, with an accompanying increase in the assumptions about the undergraduate curriculum of the teachers responsible for those grades. Those assumptions have sometimes been wildly inaccurate. When the 4th grade curriculum requires an understanding of algebra and scientific inquiry and the teacher's undergraduate preparation does not include those subjects, a challenge emerges that will not be solved with a one-day staff development course in academic standards. The teachers whose undergraduate backgrounds fail to match the standards are not bad people, nor are they unprofessional educators. Rather, their preparation is better suited to a different grade level. Effective leaders know that they should seek not to "fix" the person, but rather to find a job (and an accompanying set of standards) that best meets the teacher's abilities and background. By making decisive moves in teacher assignments, these principals saved the careers of some teachers and dramatically improved the achievement of their students.

Constructive Data Analysis. Sixth, successful schools focused intensively on student data from multiple sources, and they specifically focused on cohort data. They were less interested in comparing last year's 4th grade class with this year's 4th grade class (which, in most instances, consists of different children) and more interested in comparing the same student to the same student. Their most important question was not "Is this year's class different from last year's class?" but rather the following:

- "What percentage of a group of students is proficient now compared to a year ago?"
- "What percentage of our students have gained one or more grade levels in reading when we compare their scores today to their scores a year ago?"
- "Of those students who were not proficient a year ago, what percentage are now proficient?"
- "Of those students who were proficient a year ago, what percentage are now advanced?"

In brief, these teachers compared the students to themselves rather than to other groups of students. This analysis allowed them to focus their teaching strategies on the needs of their students and not on generic improvement methods.

Common Assessments. Seventh, the schools with the greatest improvements in student achievement consistently used common assessments. This is a dangerous recommendation to consider in an era when the most frequently heard complaint across the educational landscape is that students are overtested. To be sure, many students are overtested, but they are underassessed. The distinction between testing and assessment must be clear. Testing implies an end-of-year, summative, evaluative process in which students submit to a test and the results—typically many months later—are used by newspapers and policymakers to render a judgment about education. By the time the results are published, they are ancient history in the eyes of the student and the teacher. Contrast this to the best practice in assessment, in which students are required to complete a task and then very soon—within minutes, hours, or days—they receive feedback that is designed to improve their performance. As discussed earlier, effective assessment is what great music educators and coaches routinely provide to their students. Moreover, great educators use assessment data to make real-time decisions and to restructure their teaching accordingly. The track coach, for example, does not use the previous year's data to make decisions about assembling relay teams or selecting students to compete in the state finals. The most recent data available are far more important than the final results from the previous year. Similarly, the data from the last quarter on a school-based assessment are far more helpful than the data from last year's test. Common assessments also provide a degree of consistency in teacher expectations that is essential if fairness is our fundamental value. Although individual teachers must have discretion from day to day and hour to hour to teach, reteach, and otherwise meet the needs of individual students, they do not have the discretion to presume that their students "just can't do it." The use of a common assessment for each major discipline allows teachers to have daily discretion and independence while preserving a schoolwide commitment to equity and consistency of expectations.

The Value of Every Adult in the System. Eighth, these successful schools employed the resources of every adult in the system. In holistic accountability systems, professional development is distributed among all adults in the system. In a few notable cases, for example, every employee, including bus drivers and cafeteria workers, receives profound respect. These employees are included in professional development opportunities in classroom management and student behavior. Leaders recognize that the student's day does not really begin in the classroom, but on the bus or perhaps during free breakfast. By committing their systems to consistency in the education and behavior of adults, these leaders ensure that every staff member, from the bus driver to the food service employee to the classroom teacher, is regarded as a significant adult leader in the eyes of students. The language concerning student behavior, sanctions, and rewards is consistent, and the results are impressive. Along with gains in student achievement, these schools witnessed dramatic improvements in student behavior, including a reduction of misbehavior on buses and disciplinary incidents outside the classroom.

Holistic accountability reviews allow a consideration of extraordinary performances by all staff, including school nurses, library/media center specialists, school secretaries, custodians, counselors, psychologists, security guards, and many other unsung heroes whose exceptional efforts are disregarded in the typical accountability report. Holistic accountability does not provide a cookie-cutter approach to school success, but it does reveal the remarkable impact that every adult in the system has on student achievement.

Cross-Disciplinary Integration. Ninth, the most successful schools explicitly involve the subjects that are frequently and systematically disregarded in traditional accountability systems—music, art, physical education, world languages, technology, career education, consumer and family education, and many other variations on these themes. Analysis of holistic accountability data reveals that the involvement of these seemingly peripheral subjects in academic achievement is neither serendipitous nor insignificant. Rather, a deliberate strategy of involvement in these subjects leads to the improvement of academic results for all students. A few examples illustrate the point. Teachers meet together to review student achievement data at a deep level, including the sub-scale scores. The discussion is not that "math scores are low" but rather that "the sub-scales reveal that we need to work in particular on fractions, ratio, and measurement." This leads the music teachers to develop activities in which musical rhythms reveal the relationship of whole notes, half notes, and quarter notes. Art teachers work on perspective and other representational art that makes explicit use of scale. Physical education teachers allow students to choose to run either a millimeter or a kilometer, and when students make the wrong choice, it is a lesson most of them remember well.

In a striking example of collaboration in Norfolk, the teachers in music, art, and physical education collaborated to teach a social studies unit about African studies and the nation of Mali, the home of many of the students' ancestors. Using dance, literature, vocabulary words, geography, history, song, and engaging activities that crossed disciplinary boundaries, the teachers took the Mali unit out of its usual place in the shadows of the final week of school and infused it throughout the school year. It was hardly an accident that these students displayed astonishing improvements in their performance on state social studies tests.

Other Urban Success Stories

Norfolk is hardly an isolated example of success in urban school systems. In Indianapolis, Indiana, the Wayne Township Metropolitan School Corporation is among many that have demonstrated that academic improvement is compatible with high percentages of minority and impoverished students in the student body. In St. Louis, Missouri, Dr. Chris Wright and her colleagues have led successful initiatives in both the Riverview Gardens and Hazelwood school districts. Now, under the leadership of Dr. John Oldani and Dr. Dennis Dorsey of the Cooperating School Districts of St. Louis County, these techniques are having an impact throughout the St. Louis area. In Los Angeles County and Orange County, California, urban, suburban, and rural school systems are collaborating to create significant gains in student achievement.

The Wayne Township results are particularly interesting because they represent an example of not only successful accountability, but also the ability of a complex urban school system to replicate the success of other systems. The Wayne Township experience demonstrates that holistic accountability is not merely the result of idiosyncratic case studies, but rather the result of systematic replication of best practices from within and outside a school system. The demographic characteristics of Wayne Township might be those of any urban system, with 26 different languages spoken by the students, free and reduced lunch enrollment as high as 80 percent in some schools, and minority enrollment increasing to the point that some buildings have a majority of students from minority ethnic backgrounds. What is unusual, however, is the relentless focus of this school system on collaboration, academic standards, and nonfiction writing at every level. In particular, the years from 1999 through 2003 represent an extraordinary effort to augment the state's accountability system with a district-based holistic accountability system. In addition to the state tests, the district administers pre- and post-tests for every student in the fall and spring of each academic year. For the year ending in June 2002, every school made significant gains in mathematics and language arts. In addition, the schools with the highest poverty levels made the greatest gains, perhaps because those schools displayed the most intensive focus on changing schedules, instructional practices, building-level assessment, and leadership. It was therefore no surprise that when the state tests were administered in the fall of 2002, every building displayed significant improvement, but those buildings with the highest poverty levels displayed the greatest improvement in academic achievement. These gains exceeded 20 percent in several schools within the district.

Without a constructive accountability system in place, these results might be passed off as the temporary result of test preparation in response to pressure from state authorities. The facts contradict such a presumption. Every school in Wayne Township tracked specific practices in leadership and teaching. The schools with the greatest gains used common assessments on a monthly or quarterly basis. In addition, they routinely devoted faculty meetings and staff development sessions to collaborative scoring of student work. Each of the schools had common scoring rubrics to ensure consistent descriptions of what the word "proficient" meant in practice. Following the lead of the district, each school embraced the use of "power standards" so that teachers were able to focus on a few of the most important standards rather than every standard established by the state. This is among the most important observations of this holistic accountability study: higher test scores resulted not from mindless test prep and frantic coverage of every standard, but rather from the thoughtful application of creative and engaging teaching strategies to the most important standards.

It was noteworthy that the schools that had the greatest gains did not eliminate courses such as music, art, physical education, and technology. Rather, these courses were explicitly a part of the academic preparation of every student. In schools with the highest gains, all of the teachers in these special areas knew which standards in mathematics and language arts the students needed the most help with, and they incorporated some of those standards into their daily lessons.

Finally, the principal was personally involved in the evaluation of student work. The building leader regularly met with students and parents to discuss student achievement in specific terms. Moreover, the principal personally administered common assessments every month in language arts and math. By changing the focus of faculty meetings, the principal helped to provide additional time for collaborative scoring of student work. The principal also encouraged every teacher to prominently display proficient and exemplary student work. As a result of these displays, every student, parent, and teacher had a clear and consistent understanding of what the schoolwide scoring rubrics meant in practice.

How Holistic Accountability Affects Equity

As impressive as the improvements in academic achievement were in Wayne Township, the gains in equity were nothing short of extraordinary. Figure 5.1 represents the typical relationship between poverty and student achievement. As the graph indicates, the higher the level of poverty, the lower the level of student achievement. The line extending from the upper left to the lower right shows that as the percentage of students in poverty (as defined by those eligible for free or reduced lunch) increases, the achievement (as measured by test scores) decreases. This relationship is not perfectly negative (-1.0), but it is substantial in most national research, ranging from -.6 to -.9. The prevailing assertion in more than four decades of research on the topic is that variables such as student poverty account for 90 percent or more of the variation in student test scores (Marzano, 2003). If we stop after considering Figure 5.1, then these prevailing assertions will carry the day. The accountability evidence, however, suggests that specific teaching, leadership, and curriculum strategies will mitigate the impact of poverty.

Figures 5.2 through 5.5 indicate that the negative relationship between student poverty and student achievement is not a certainty in Wayne Township. Although Figure 5.4 shows that the district's grade 6 language arts scores are disappointingly negative (-.35), the overall relationship between poverty and achievement is far less than is the case nationally, and in three out of four examples (grade 3 language arts and math, and grade 6 math), the relationships are almost flat. In other words, this school system has demonstrated that the relationship between poverty and student achievement can be negligible.

Figure 5.4 shows that for students in the middle grades in language arts, the equity gap remains a concern, measured at -.35. Nevertheless, compare this chart to Figure 5.1, where the national average of the relationship between student achievement and free and reduced-price lunch eligibility is -.6 to -.9. This district has not closed the equity gap, but it has significantly reduced it. Figure 5.5

Figure 5.1

Poverty and Student Proficiency: The National Norm

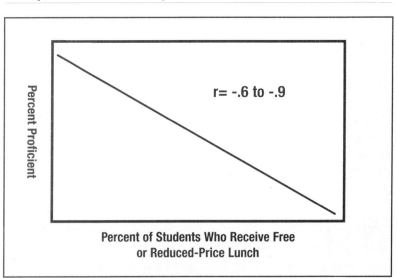

Figure 5.2

**Relationship Between Poverty and Student Proficiency
in Grade 3 Language Arts in Wayne Township**

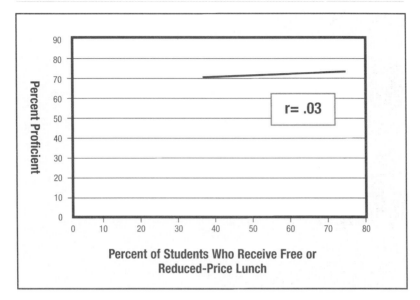

Figure 5.3

**Relationship Between Poverty and Student Proficiency
in Grade 3 Mathematics in Wayne Township**

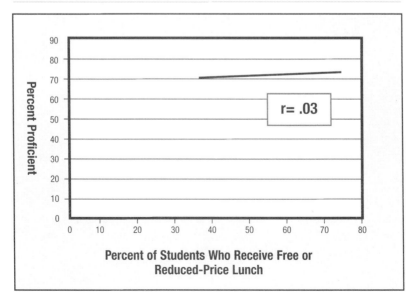

Figure 5.4

Relationship Between Poverty and Student Proficiency in Grade 6 Language Arts in Wayne Township

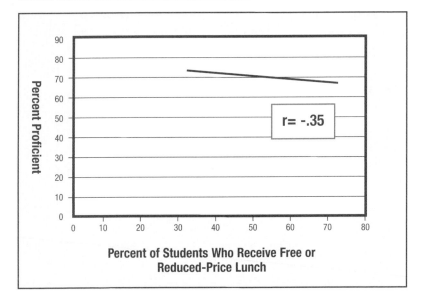

Figure 5.5

Relationship Between Poverty and Student Proficiency in Grade 6 Mathematics in Wayne Township

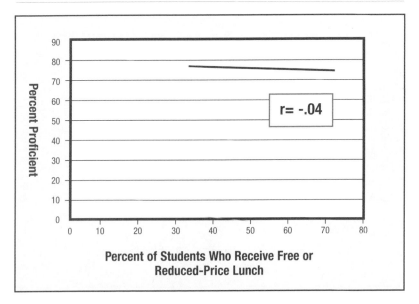

is interesting because these are the same students as Figure 5.4, where the equity gap was -.35. Why is the math gap almost zero while the language arts gap is -.35? One possible explanation is that middle school math is a subject matter most likely to be taught in school and very likely to be taught at home. Student proficiency in reading and writing, by contrast, is often a combination of the impact of home and school environments. This chart provides very encouraging data for teachers—those subjects taught in school can have a profound impact on closing the equity gap.

The Wayne Township experience shows that equity need not be a dream. Every single building in the district—elementary through high school—achieved one of the following two equity indicators: (1) the difference in achievement between students eligible for free and reduced lunch and the average was less than 10 percent, or (2) the difference in achievement between the largest minority group of students and the average was less than 10 percent. These data points are totally consistent with the improvements in equity in Milwaukee, Wisconsin; Freeport, Illinois; Riverview Gardens (St. Louis, Missouri, metropolitan area); and other districts. Although no one disputes that poverty, linguistic differences, and culture can be important variables influencing student achievement, the research is clear that variables in teaching, curriculum, and leadership are profoundly important. In fact, these variables—which teachers and leaders can control—have more influence over student achievement than the intractable variables of poverty, culture, and language.

Addressing the Cynics and Critics

We must take a few minutes to address the inevitable critics who seem constitutionally unable to believe that a success story in urban education exists. Whenever I share results such as those in Norfolk, Wayne Township, Milwaukee, Riverview Gardens, Freeport, and other successful urban school systems, critics inevitably roll their eyes and allege that this surely must be a flash in the pan, the product of a frenzy of test preparation rather than sustainable reform. Others claim that the results must be due to the exclusion of underperforming children on test day. Still other critics claim that the students and teachers must be engaged in a massive cheating conspiracy. Others take issue with the methodology of the research, particularly if careful research controls (such as mobility and attendance) are used. The presence of those controls inflates achievement, the critics charge. After all, the studies reflect students who actually attend school. Of course, the absence of those controls would lead to charges of sloppy research. Either way, the critics find a way to ignore the growing pile of research. The researcher who documents high achievement in poor schools cannot win when the argumentative deck is thus stacked.

When all of the allegations about the quantity and quality of research are refuted, the critics do not yield, but simply declare they do not believe it. The critics, who claim to be defenders and friends of public education, appear to be incapable of acknowledging the possibility that poor and minority children can make academic progress under the guidance of professional and hard-working educators. I am used to these allegations, having heard charges against other cases in which I have documented the success of students in high-poverty, high-minority schools (Reeves, 2000a). This is a little different from the arguments over research done in previous decades by the late Ron Edmonds or more recent evidence supplied by The Education Trust, Inc. (Jerald, 2001). Critics simply do not believe it.

A charitable view would regard the criticism as the "doubting Thomas" effect—when research seems extraordinary and not in keeping with one's own experience, then the skeptic must have multiple sources of evidence and replicated examples of the research in order to overcome the doubts. This is a reasoned view, worthy of good students of research. But how to explain the skeptics' persistence even after providing them with multiple sources of evidence over many years? A less charitable explanation is what I term the "infantilizing" of education policy discussions. Infants do not care about research reports. If they see an object, it exists. If they cover their eyes, the object disappears. If the object is covered by another object, then only after a few more months of cognitive development will they grasp that both objects remain present. In early infancy, the concealed object might as well have disappeared. We do not debate with infants or get angry with them, but patiently wait for the infants' cognitive skills to develop. Even when infants make noises that are shrill and unpleasant, we tolerate it, knowing that a better day will come. Readers serving urban schools with a commitment to higher achievement would be well advised to consider this metaphor when dealing with their inevitable critics. Do not be angry, defensive, or lured into rhetorical baiting. Do not allow the noise, however unpleasant, to divert you from the mission of excellence and equity for your students. The quality of your work and that of your students will, in time, speak louder than the wailing of your critics.

As noted earlier, Norfolk, Virginia, and Wayne Township Metropolitan School District in Indianapolis are examples that defy the critics' presumptions. But we can point to other districts as well. Milwaukee Public Schools has demonstrated the value of accountability, standards, and common assessments. Despite a succession of different leaders, the vagaries of board politics, and exceptionally difficult financial and policy constraints, this remarkable public school system has consistently improved student achievement and equity for more than 100,000 students. In Los Angeles County, the headlines are dominated by what goes wrong. Nevertheless, careful observers note that both in the nation's second largest school system, Los Angeles Unified School District, and in other districts in Los Angeles County, significant gains in reading have occurred where principals and teachers have followed the same principles that were successful in Norfolk and other urban areas. In metropolitan St. Louis County, specific successes can be documented in districts such as Riverview Gardens and Hazelwood, where neither poverty nor minority enrollment has diminished the commitment of teachers and leaders to improved student achievement.

In urban Atlanta, the Cobb County school system has demonstrated a little-noticed commitment to equity as its student writing scores have contradicted the typical negative relationship that most observers presume—the greater the poverty level, the lower the test scores. Cobb County has dramatically reduced the impact of that relationship with regard to student writing. Although there remains a negative relationship between student proficiency in reading and poverty, such a relationship is absent with regard to student proficiency in writing. This suggests that writing, a skill more likely to be taught in school, has the potential to mitigate the impact of poverty. This is consistent with the data in Lee County, Florida, where the relationship between student poverty and writing scores is much less negative than the relationship between poverty and early reading scores. In other words, what happens in school matters, and it particularly matters when it comes to mitigating the effects of poverty.

No review of urban school systems would be complete without a consideration of New York City, which, pundits claim, is the proverbial black hole of educational reform—money and ideas go in, but they never come out. Let the facts, for a moment, interfere with preconceptions. Professor Lucy McCormick Calkins of Columbia University has devoted a professional lifetime to debunking presumptions about what students can and cannot do. When she shares examples of the work of public school students (Calkins, 1983, 1994), the ironic response is, "They must be gifted." To be sure, they are, Professor Calkins notes, and so is every child who is given the opportunity to succeed and who benefits from the relentless demands of teachers who accept nothing less than exemplary work from students.

The common theme for these success stories is that the educators involved do not merely examine test scores, but rather engage in a deeper consideration of accountability for every participant in the educational system. To be sure, test scores are a part of these considerations, but for accountability to reach its potential as a constructive force in education, it must include explicit acknowledgment of the role that every adult—from the classroom teacher to the bus driver to the central office administrator to the superintendent to the board of education member—plays in improving student achievement and educational equity.

6

The Policymaker's Perspective

No discussion of educational accountability would be complete without a consideration of the educational policymaker at the federal, state, and local levels. In the early years of the 21st century, the federal government has become involved in educational accountability in an unprecedented manner. The No Child Left Behind Act, passed by large majorities of both political parties, represents an exceptional degree of federal influence in curriculum, teaching, research, leadership, and other areas of educational policy. Unfortunately, much of the commentary on the law has been so politically and emotionally charged that it is increasingly difficult to conduct a rational (and civil) discussion of the matter. This chapter brackets a discussion of the myths and realities of federal policy with considerations of the impact of policymakers at the local and state levels. Although much of the publicity surrounding state-level accountability plans is focused on federal legislation, local and state policymakers remain enormously influential in the establishment of educational policy.

The Local Role: School Board Policies in Accountability

One can hardly blame school boards (and, depending on the local governance structure, school committees, county commissions, city councils, and other governing bodies) for feeling as if their powers have been diminished in the past several years. Elements of school policy, such as curriculum, academic content, assessment, promotion, and graduation, all of which were formerly under the exclusive control of the local school system, have recently become dictated by state departments of education. Those state departments, in turn, complain that their mandates merely reflect a national trend in legislative reforms at the state and national levels, the cumulative effect of which is more accountability in public education.

Local school boards are hardly impotent, and the following paragraphs address some of the most important issues in education over which boards must exercise more diligent policy control. Indeed, the best intentions of state and federal policy will go awry if policies adopted at the local level do not include assiduous implementation of improved opportunities for all students.

Teacher Quality

School boards approve contracts with teachers' unions and other bargaining groups. Although most of the attention in these documents has been devoted to financial matters, these contracts also contain local policies that dramatically affect teacher quality and students' opportunity to learn. As a result of some local policies, the assignment of teachers to buildings, grade levels, and courses is a matter of seniority. Teachers with the most seniority have the highest priority in choosing where they teach and what they teach. Although on the surface this may seem to be a simple reflection of RHIP—rank has its privileges—the effect on student achievement and opportunity to learn has been pernicious. In many cases, the teachers with the most experience gravitate toward schools with the least number of disadvantaged students. Within schools, the most experienced teachers choose to teach courses with the least number of disadvantaged students. This leaves students who have the greatest need with the least experienced and, in many cases, the least qualified teachers (Ingersoll, 2003).

Teachers are hardly to blame for this state of affairs; they are simply exercising their rights secured through collective bargaining. It is the local school boards that must bear responsibility for approving these contracts, and the local school boards must negotiate alternatives. The best practices are the provision of economic and noneconomic incentives (more time, fewer students, more technology support, more safety support) for teachers who are willing to serve in the schools and the classes with the greatest numbers of disadvantaged students. When boards merely announce policies about high standards and tough accountability systems but fail to give students the opportunity for a quality teacher in the classroom, the policies are hollow rhetoric.

Teacher quality is not merely a matter of experience and certification, of course. The most effective teachers and school leaders use strikingly different professional practices. Boards must have an evaluation system that is more than a bureaucratic stamp reflecting what teachers did outside the classroom and must instead embrace every opportunity to recognize and reward exceptional teacher effectiveness inside the classroom. This includes not only recognition, but also specific economic and noneconomic rewards. We know that feedback in student achievement must be timely, accurate, and specific (Marzano, Pickering, & Pollock, 2001), yet few interactions between boards, senior leaders, and classroom educators could meet these criteria for effective feedback. Far more than the retirement apples and "teacher of the year" awards, successful feedback systems must provide opportunities for every single educator and leader in the system to identify, document, and replicate their most effective practices. If accountability for learning, as described in these pages, is to have an effect on the school system, then it is the board that must legitimate an approach to accountability that is more than a litany of test scores. Bluntly stated, teacher quality will be an accident rather than the result of careful design if board accountability systems fail to identify, document, recognize, and reward quality on multiple levels throughout the system.

Part of maintaining quality is the identification and replacement of employees who fail to meet the standards of the school board. Unfortunately, most teacher terminations happen amid great controversy and acrimony, and too many are associated with such gross malfeasance, such as criminal behavior with students, that there is little question of discretion by the school district leadership. The use of quality controls for teachers whose behavior is inadequate rather than felonious is a much more difficult matter. Some of the most successful models of performance improvement, including alternatives to removing teachers from the job, have been sponsored by the two largest teachers unions, the American Federation of Teachers and the National Education Association (see http://www.aft.org and http://www.nea.org for the latest information on teacher improvement from a union perspective). Fundamentally, teachers want to be successful and know that every incompetent teacher reflects badly on the entire profession. But the label of "incompetent" cannot be assigned without due process and opportunities for improvement. Teaching skills are not embedded in one's DNA, but can be learned, practiced, and improved. Some teachers have been ineffective at one grade level or position, but, given the opportunity to move to another grade level where the teacher's background more closely matches the material being taught, a prospective failure can be turned into a successful professional. At the end of the day, however, every board must have a process in place that allows not only for termination for gross malfeasance and for the removal of new and untenured teachers, but also for the identification and documentation of inadequate performance and, ultimately, the reassignment or removal of educators and leaders who fail to meet the board's standards.

These two contrasting themes—identification of teacher strengths and intolerance of incompetent teaching—do not deserve equal weight. As a cardinal principle of leadership, it is faster and easier to build on strengths than to compensate for weaknesses (Buckingham & Clifton, 2001). Board members and senior leaders must devote far more energy to the identification of teaching strengths and the systematic replication of those strengths than to removing their least competent teachers.

Strategic Planning

Too many boards have become enmeshed in the processes of strategic planning, as if the production of strategic planning documents were the end of the enterprise. The most important role of the board in strategic planning is focus, ensuring that the plan and all that it implies are consistent with the board's mission and vision. Too many strategic planning processes are cumulative, collecting ideas from multiple stakeholders (a good idea) and then ensuring that each of these stakeholders feels that his or her voice is heard by having a particular initiative inserted in the strategic plan (a terrible idea). When boards are focused, they have very few goals. In the case of Norfolk Public Schools, highlighted in Chapter 5, the board had a single goal. It is no accident that in successful school systems we have evaluated, we almost always find fewer than half a dozen board goals, and the meaning of those goals is remarkably clear.

Commitment to effective strategic planning is evident in many decisions that board members make that do not bear a label resembling anything like "strategic planning." The items of the agenda, the correspondence among members, the budget decisions (particularly decisions to stop unproductive activities and to discontinue unhelpful programs), the organization of the central office, and the way that senior leaders are evaluated are all evidence of how the board is, or is not, reflecting its purported strategy in its daily decision making.

Leadership Evaluation

One of the most important things that boards do is to evaluate leaders—particularly the superintendent of schools. In a recent study I conducted with my colleagues at the Center for Performance Assessment (Reeves, 2003a), 18 percent of school leaders had never been evaluated in their present position, and only a minority of those who had been evaluated believed that the evaluations were related to student achievement and were sufficiently specific to allow the leaders to improve their performance. Worst of all, the higher the position, the worse the quality of the evaluations.

Therefore, a substantial need exists for school board members to devote significantly more attention than is often the case to the development of a constructive evaluation process for superintendents and senior leaders. Specifically, the board's evaluation should identify dimensions of leadership most important for that position, as well as a continuum of performance (from "not meeting standards" to "exemplary") for each dimension of leadership. Although each board will craft its evaluation policies based on local needs and culture, a model that boards may wish to consider appears in the book *Assessing Educational Leaders* (Reeves, 2003a). Samples of the leadership dimensions can be downloaded free of charge from the Web site http://www.MakingStandardsWork.com. In addition, Marzano offers exceptional insight into the critical role of leadership in Chapter 18 of his landmark work *What Works in Schools: Translating Research into Action* (Marzano, 2003).

Public Engagement

Boards of education and other local governing structures are inherently political. Whether filling an appointed or elected position, each board member serves a set of constituents, many of whom have conflicting agendas and interests. These agendas and interests are influenced by a stream of information from multiple sources, many of which are also starkly in conflict. Board members are bombarded day and night (because I am married to a school board member, I speak with some authority on this point) with information from people claiming the absolute truth as a result of a news report, a casual conversation with a school employee, a report from a student, an allegation from a talk-radio host, a conversation with another board member, or any number of informal and formal sources. Although the deluge of information is one of the wonders and burdens of a free society, it also imposes on board members the obligation to become educators themselves, not merely announcing policies, but also educating their many constituencies about the truth behind their reasoning in the establishment of such policies. This is a lesson that senior school leaders should well remember as they announce and implement new school board policies. In a phrase, "why" precedes "how." The obligation of school board members and senior leaders is not merely to announce their decisions. They must also fully engage their employees, the public, and other constituents and explain the reasoning—including relevant research, public interests, local cultural issues, and other factors—that influenced the "why" of the decision-making process. Only when these issues have been fully addressed will an audience even consider the "how" part of the equation.

We have heard unending allegations about the "loss of local control" in education for decades, yet every school board member I have observed is extraordinarily busy and committed. Those who have served in other public offices, including executive and legislative positions, recall school board service as that involving the most complexity, the most stress, and the greatest impact on the daily lives of their constituents. Although the shifting tide of national policy in education does significantly broaden the role of the federal and state levels of government, local school boards remain the primary policy link that determines the extent to which national and state visions of student excellence and equity will be illusions or realities.

The Federal Role: Myths and Realities About No Child Left Behind

Although a comprehensive analysis of federal education legislation is beyond the scope of this book, what follows is a brief review of some of the comments regarding reauthorization of the Elementary and Secondary Education Act in 2001, enacted as House Resolution Number 1, the No Child Left Behind Act. Although I am an advocate for educational standards as a methodology vastly superior to the bell curve (Reeves, 2001b), I have also been quite critical of standardized testing (Reeves, 2000b). In addition, I have attempted to take an evenhanded and nonpartisan stance in a review of the educational policies advocated by President Bush and the leaders of the Democratic Party (Reeves, 2001a). The following discussion of myths and realities is neither a defense nor a condemnation of the No Child Left Behind Act, but rather an attempt to focus the discussion on facts rather than the politically charged rhetoric that has dominated so much of the discussion of this law since its enactment. The labels of "liberal" and "conservative" are excessively broad and imprecise, and thus I am painting with broad brushstrokes in the following paragraphs. These descriptions characterizing the opposition to federal education law do not diminish the sincerity or good intentions of any of these groups, but serve only to illustrate the widely different perspectives of the opposition groups. The opposition to the bill comes from a curious combination of sources, including the following:

- Teachers and administrators who sincerely want to improve student achievement but are feeling overwhelmed by the number of new requirements imposed on them in the past several years.

- Traditionally conservative political activists who believe that the federal government has no right to impose its will in the field of education. In some cases, this opposition extends not only to federal requirements for state academic standards and reading tests, but also to federal involvement in civil rights, including the rights of disabled students and the rights of female students to participate equitably in sports.

- Traditionally liberal political activists who believe that any testing program will hurt poor and minority students.

- Parent groups in upper-middle-class neighborhoods who fear that an emphasis on testing in reading and mathematics will detract from special programs and electives that their children enjoy and are entitled to.

The No Child Left Behind Act certainly enjoys support among many other interest groups. Unfortunately, neither side in the debate will advance the cause of reason by challenging the motives, intelligence, or good will of its opponents.

Myth: The No Child Left Behind Act Is the "Bush Bill"

More than 90 percent of Democratic U.S. senators and representatives voted in favor of this law. Some of the most important amendments to the law were authored by Senator Hillary Rodham Clinton

of New York, and the bill was ushered through the Senate commit-
tee chaired by Senator Edward Kennedy of Massachusetts. The day
the bill was signed, a bipartisan congressional delegation, including
Senator Kennedy, toured the country with President Bush to praise
the contents of the bill. Although we are all free to take potshots at
the politician of our choice, simple fairness demands that our criticisms of the No Child Left Behind Act be bipartisan.

Myth: Nationally Standardized Tests Are Required by Federal Law

The No Child Left Behind Act explicitly *prohibits* the use of a
nationally standardized test. In fact, it requires each state to develop
tests in reading and mathematics for students in grades 3 through 8.
Those tests must be based on state standards, not federal requirements. Moreover, the content, form, and timing of those assessments are matters left to state discretion. States have exceptionally
wide latitude in assessment policy, with some states using traditional off-the-shelf multiple-choice tests and other states creating
tests at the local level. Some states have engaged corporate testing
giants to create their tests, whereas other states use consortia of uni-
versities and classroom educators. Some states have standardized
conditions for testing throughout the state, and other states allow a
wide degree of local discretion.

What is remarkable so far is the number of states that are
"overcomplying" with the testing provisions of the No Child Left
Behind Act. Federal requirements mandate only that schools
must know the degree to which students meet reading and math
standards once a year. One wonders if any school in the nation
was not already conducting such an inquiry. Many states have
developed testing regimens in many other subjects and thus far
exceed the requirements of the federal law. My informal interviews with teachers throughout the nation reveal that time
requirements for state tests range from a couple of hours of testing to almost 40 hours of testing. This high level of variation
should make it clear that it is state government, not the U.S.
Department of Education, that is making the most significant
decisions when it comes to testing of students.

Myth: The Right of Children to Leave Failing Schools Is a Republican Party Ploy to Support Vouchers and Charter Schools

Although I cannot speculate on the motives of the law's authors, I can report on two salient facts. First, the signature that appears on Executive Order 13153, which authorizes parents to move students out of schools that receive federal funds and that fail to make adequate progress for two consecutive years, is not that of George W. Bush. That executive order, signed in May 2000, bears the signature of President Bill Clinton, rarely regarded by critics of federal law as an enemy of public education. Second, although the original language of the No Child Left Behind Act included a provision for vouchers, that section of the bill was quickly designated as "dead on arrival" in Congress and never made it past the congressional committees to which it was assigned for hearings. The present law provides choice within the public system, including choices among public schools and choices to attend publicly funded charter schools in those states that have authorized such schools.

Myth: The Law's Requirements Will Replace Thinking and Analysis with Low-Level Thinking Skills

It is true that the reaction of some states (and, to be sure, the reactions of some principals and teachers) to the No Child Left Behind Act has been an excessive focus on test preparation, a good deal of which is little more than an ill-conceived repetition of practice test questions. The critics are rightly indignant at such poor pedagogy, but their indignation should be aimed in the right direction. Even if the state test is dominated by lower-level thinking skills and questions are posed in a multiple-choice format, the best preparation for such tests is not mindless testing drills, but extensive student writing, accompanied by thinking, analysis, and reasoning (Reeves, 2002d). Moreover, the federal law requires only that states use tests based upon their own academic content standards. Some states have embraced standards that are rich in analytical reasoning and complex thinking requirements. A state's failure to adopt such standards and to match its assessments to these requirements for thinking, analysis, reasoning, and writing is a failure in the state capital, not in Washington, D.C.

Before the chorus of voices that demean "drill and kill" is allowed to pass without challenge, we must recognize the plain fact that students *do* need to learn to read and to analyze basic mathematical problems to function in society. Learning the names, shapes, and sounds of letters along with the meaning of words is, at times, a drill, as is learning to shoot a basketball, play the saxophone, or clean one's room. Not every drill is deadly and without purpose. However dull the reading and math curriculum may be, it is only fair to note that it is preferable to a curriculum characterized by low expectations and content that is fragmentary, idiosyncratic, and incoherent. The broader issue, however, is that the law explicitly refers to broadly based academic standards created at the *state* level.

Myth: The Law Ignores the Needs of Students with Disabilities

The Individuals with Disabilities Education Act (IDEA) is a separate piece of legislation from the No Child Left Behind Act. The former guarantees to students with disabilities the federally protected right to assessments that are fair and appropriate based on their individual needs. Where state tests are inappropriate, students with disabilities must be afforded the opportunity to engage in appropriate alternative assessments. I have heard several times the assertion that a child who is unable to read must sit, invariably in tears, in front of a test for hours at a time, and that such a state of affairs is the result of the No Child Left Behind Act. If such stories are not apocryphal, then it is the fault of testing administrators at the state and local level who have elevated rumor over fact. A significant body of legislative, administrative, and case law supports the rights of disabled students to appropriate assessments, and the No Child Left Behind Act does not repeal a scintilla of those protections. Indeed, the implementing regulations for the No Child Left Behind Act, published in July of 2002, specifically require that state assessments "be designed to be valid and accessible for use with the widest possible range of students, including students with disabilities and students with limited English proficiency" (U.S. Department of Education, 2002).

Myth: Standardized Test Scores Are All That Matter

Much of the attention given to this law in its early days has been focused on the requirements for testing students in grades 3 through 8 in reading and math, a requirement that will be extended to include testing in science by 2007. This chapter addresses the specifics of new federal legislation and the impact on accountability. Contrary to popular myth, the No Child Left Behind Act does not rely exclusively on standardized test scores to define student progress, and exceptional opportunities for flexibility and balance in educational accountability are available for those states and districts willing to take advantage of them. Nebraska Commissioner of Education Douglas Christenson has made it clear that his state will not settle for single-measurement accountability; Nebraska neatly balances standardized test data with assessments chosen by local school systems and classroom evaluations (2001).

Teacher Quality and No Child Left Behind

Although most of the focus on the federal legislation has been directed to the testing of students in reading and mathematics, an equally important part of the law is the requirement that a "highly qualified" teacher must be placed in all classrooms. Although the definition of "highly qualified" has been left to the states, it is almost certain that this definition implies the requirement that teachers have more formal training in the subject matters that they teach. The clear legislative intent of the No Child Left Behind Act is to put an end to "out-of-field" teaching, in which the physical education teacher is required to teach a government class and the driver's education instructor must teach a section of algebra. This problem has been particularly acute in the nation's poorest school systems, where students are far more likely to be taught by an out-of-field teacher than is the case in schools where students are economically advantaged (Ingersoll, 2003).

The legal and policy emphasis on teacher quality is important, because it explicitly acknowledges what the research says: teacher quality is the most important single influence on student achievement

(Marzano, 2003; Reeves, 2002d; Sanders, 1998). The challenge facing policymakers will be to avoid the dilution of the term "highly qualified teacher" to mean nothing more than "person who has purchased a credential." In the Vietnam War era, when deferments were offered to members of the clergy, the mail-order divinity degree became a necessary accoutrement of some people wishing to avoid military service. Forty years later, the Internet degree in education may be the quick alternative to those wishing to avoid an undergraduate curriculum that includes the challenges posed by a classroom environment. Despite the advent of many successful and worthwhile Internet-based training programs, the unalterable fact remains that one does not learn to deal with a classroom of real students without spending time with real students. Moreover, one does not learn to convey complex content to real students by answering questions on a test about how one might respond in a theoretical circumstance, but rather by interacting with the complex web of highly variable interests, motivations, and backgrounds that are the daily reality of the classroom.

The Individuals with Disabilities Education Act and No Child Left Behind

In 2003 Congress was considering significant modifications to the Individuals with Disabilities Education Act, one of the most important civil rights laws of the latter part of the 20th century. Although federally established protections for students with disabilities have been on the books since the early 1970s, a persistent gap separates federal expectations and reality. Part of that gap is due to the funding dilemma in which federal law creates mandates for appropriate education of special education students in the "least restrictive environment," yet the government fails to come close to providing enough financial assistance to states and local school districts to meet the letter and spirit of that requirement. Moreover, an inherent tension exists between state testing policies designed to ensure adequate inclusion of special education students and the protections in IDEA that require the individualization of curriculum and assessment for those students. In some cases, state imperatives for universal standardized testing of all students, including special education students, directly contradict federal requirements that assessment must be based on the individual needs of each student. For some students, state standardized tests are far from appropriate, and for a few students, exclusion from testing may be the proper approach. The tension between these various state and federal requirements will inevitably be settled in the courts, leaving local school districts in a quandary over whether funds that should have been devoted to education must now be devoted to litigation.

The State Role

Since the earliest days of the Republic, education has been a local matter. What "local control" really means in practice, however, continues to be subject to considerable debate. According to the 10th Amendment to the United States Constitution, the governmental powers not specifically addressed in that document are reserved for the states. Because education is not addressed in the federal document, it has historically been a matter governed by the states. Some of the original colonies, such as Massachusetts, created a state constitutional right to an adequate education. The primary author of the Massachusetts state constitution, John Adams, was also acutely aware of the omission of this subject from both the Articles of Confederation and the U.S. Constitution, and thus ensured its prominence in the state constitution. The influence of the federal government in education is strictly a matter of money rather than constitutionally granted power. If a state is willing to reject federal funding (typically from 5 to 20 percent of the total budget of a school system, depending on the demographic characteristics of its student population), then the state can be liberated from many federal requirements. Only those federal requirements based on the "equal protection" clause of the 14th Amendment to the U.S. Constitution, such as protection from discrimination on account of race or sex, or protections based on the First Amendment, preventing the "establishment" of a religion, are enforceable whether or not a state receives federal funds.

Although the No Child Left Behind Act has been described as the largest imposition of federal control over education in the nation's history, the plain fact is that the state implementing the regulations will have an enormous impact on how the federal law affects individual students and schools. Moreover, the state implementation plans that have been approved by the U.S. Department of Education show enormous variation. Standards vary widely from state to state, as does the definition of "adequate yearly progress." In some cases, progress must occur in a linear fashion—that is, if a 50 percent gain must occur over 10 years, then the state has decreed a 5 percent gain per year as the indicator of acceptable progress. Other states, such as Ohio, have taken a nonlinear approach, and a substantial amount of their "adequate yearly progress" will not be required until the years after 2010. The common criticisms of the definitions of adequate progress are more appropriately directed to the state, rather than the federal government.

The End of "Local Control"

States have the exclusive authority to decide what their academic standards will be, how they govern curriculum and assessment, and how they describe student achievement. The state government is clearly the dominant force in educational policy, yet enormous tension remains between states and local school systems. Even in the Commonwealth of Massachusetts in the 21st century, confusion and seemingly endless litigation occur on two points:

- What does "adequate education" really mean?
- Does "local control" mean the state government or the local school governing body?

Because local school boards have traditionally enjoyed broad latitude to make policy on everything from student discipline to textbook selection to the criteria for high school diplomas, the recent imposition of state standards and state-mandated assessments represents an enormous erosion of local school system authority. In addition, local school systems in several states, such as Kansas, Arkansas, and Pennsylvania, where entire school districts may have fewer than 500 students, are now being forced by financial limitations to consider consolidation and power sharing with other districts. Thus the tradition of local control is suffering multiple challenges:

- The state, not the local school board, is determining academic content through the imposition of state standards.

- The state, not the local school board, is determining high school graduation requirements.

- The regions within a state, including longtime rivals, are being forced to consolidate or at least to cooperate in the provision of administrative services. This is particularly troublesome when schools consolidate and a local community loses its civic anchor—the local high school.

- The criteria for evaluating educational leaders and teachers are no longer the judgments of the local superintendent and the governing board, but the criteria for educational quality established by the state. This is particularly important in regard to indicators of teacher quality, as that most local of decisions—who teaches which classes—is no longer a matter for the local building principal or superintendent to decide.

Despite the erosion of local control, the states and local school systems retain some of the most important decision-making authority in education. Federal legislation grants very broad discretion to the states on everything from the establishment of state academic standards to the qualifications for high school graduation. Even terms that are contained in federal statute, such as "adequate yearly progress" in education, are defined in widely varying ways by the states. Some states require schools to make a defined increment of progress each year, whereas other states allow less progress in early years and expect greater progress in later years. Some states set a very high bar for "proficiency" and thus accept the pejorative labels that inevitably ensue when a substantial number of students and schools fail to meet such a high standard. Other states, by contrast, define acceptable levels of performance much lower, so that virtually every school will meet the state standard and thus avoid the obloquy of the state department of education and the press.

Although each state decision-making pattern has its critics and defenders, the inescapable fact is that these are state, not federal, decisions. Local school boards, mayors, county officials, and other policymakers at the local level can exert much more meaningful influence over educational policy if they focus their efforts on state, rather than federal, governmental affairs.

The Role of State Leaders in Accountability for Learning

With the passage of the No Child Left Behind Act, educational policymakers at the state level have an unprecedented opportunity to have a profound impact on the quality and equity of schools. The federal law provides a significant degree of flexibility, and the best evidence for this flexibility is the exceptional variety of strategies in the various state plans that have already been approved by the U.S. Department of Education. As noted, some plans define "adequate yearly progress" in a linear manner, while other states take a nonlinear approach, with very little progress required in the early years of program implementation, but substantially high degrees of progress required later. Some states explicitly include student mobility controls and attendance controls in their definitions of adequate yearly progress. Some states are requiring extensive performance assessments with a particular emphasis on student writing, while other states focus more on multiple-choice tests. In brief, the preliminary impact of the No Child Left Behind Act is emphatically not a "one size fits all" program of federal legislation, but rather an astonishing variety of different ideas from the 50 states. The degree to which state flexibility will be meaningful is a judgment on which the jury has yet to render a verdict. Some states will use their new flexibility to engage in bold new initiatives (Christensen, 2001) and others will merely replace the bureaucracy of Washington, D.C., for one located in their state capital. In the latter cases, the flexibility and local control that were hoped for as a result of a shift from federal to state control will be largely illusory.

The Central Challenge for State Governments: Constructive Accountability

Despite the federal requirements for state governments to report test scores in reading, math, and (eventually) science, every state has the opportunity to make their accountability systems far more than a set of box scores containing test numbers. A state that embraced the student-centered accountability presented in this book would learn more than what the scores are, and would conduct a deeper inquiry into the resources, curriculum, teaching, and leadership of schools. Only with such a holistic view of accountability will state departments of education understand that two schools with identical test scores can be vastly different places of learning.

Distinctions Without a Difference: The Fallacy of State Grades

When researchers claim to have found a difference between two measurements that is not really meaningful (such as a body temperature variation from 98.6 to 98.5), they do not claim that the body temperature of the patient is plummeting and that drastic action is required. Rather they recognize that a certain amount of normal variation occurs within any human system, and that not every distinction in numbers represents a meaningful difference. This lesson is lost on state policymakers who insist on allowing minute numerical distinctions to cause enormous differences in school labels. Even some of the best accountability systems in the country have fallen prey to the public demand for the assignment of letter grades to schools. Decades of research in classroom assessment have helped us understand the errors that inevitably creep into the use of a single letter to represent a complex set of variables. One student, for example, might receive a *B-* because her work was submitted late, though she met every academic standard. Another student, by contrast, submits work that does not meet standards, but does so with a cheerful attitude, compliant behavior, and unfailing timeliness. His reward is the same *B-*, and parents are left to wonder, "What in the world do grades really mean?" Similarly, states that use grades (or categories, or other labels) depend upon a single letter or word to represent a universe of variables that is far more complex. As I write this chapter, I am aware of a school where the difference between an acceptable and unacceptable grade came down to the performance of one student in one grade. If the technical rules required inclusion of that student, the school would fail. If the technical rules (in this case, on mobility) allowed exclusion of that student's score, the school would succeed. The difference in the schoolwide average represents only a fraction of a percentage point, but it is all the difference in the world for the jobs and professional self-respect of the administrators and teachers in this building.

Ironically, this has the opposite impact desired by state policymakers. Rather than creating a system that is more rigorous with high expectations for all students, administrators can figure out how to game the system. I have heard administrators in an open forum, for example, claim that their strategy is to work on students "on the bubble"—that is, within a few points of passing—rather than work on the lowest-performing students. After all, if the state only cares about the "percentage of students who are proficient or higher" and the proficiency threshold is a score of 70, then they find little point in working to move a student from a score of 20 to a score of 60. No matter how enormous an achievement that might be, it is valueless in a system that only shows the growth in the percentage of students whose scores exceed 70.

Guidelines for State Policymakers

• **Measure student progress comprehensively.** While "percentage of students proficient or higher" is an important measurement for standards-based systems, it need not be the only measurement. Additional measurements that may be appropriate include the percentage of students making one or more grade levels of academic progress since the previous year's assessment, and the percentage of students advancing one or more category of proficiency (for example, from not meeting standards to progressing, or from progressing to proficient, or from proficient to advanced) since the previous year's assessment.

• **Measure the antecedents of excellence.** The state can create a menu of indicators in teaching, curriculum, leadership, extracurricular

activities, and other school-based factors that are explicitly related
to improved student achievement. In this supplementary report,
schools choose five or six indicators that are most important for
them. Each selection of a school-based indicator represents that
school's hypothesis that such a strategy will be related to that
school's academic progress. The insights arising from this report not
only help schools understand which strategies work best for them,
but in the aggregate, these indicators from around the state create a
research gold mine for state policymakers.

• **Provide a mix of quantitative and qualitative evidence.** Narrative descriptions of school climate, triumphs, and tragedies can
provide an important qualitative lens through which quantitative data
can be better understood. Although every school may use the identical state test, there are unique characteristics of each school that a
one-page qualitative description can make clear. Because of the massive quantity of state accountability data, it is easy for policymakers
and citizens alike to fall prey to the temptation to summarize vast
amounts of numbers with a simple box score. With so many schools
to consider, how can we possible consider the characteristics of each
school on an individual basis? Here we should be guided by Ein-
stein's maxim that "things should be made as simple as possible, but
not more so." While a state education executive, board member, or
legislator may not be able to read every narrative description for
every school, the availability of these descriptions allows policy ana-
lysts at every level to consider the "story behind the numbers." Consider the daily newspaper, where the sports and business pages
routinely recognize that the game scores and stock prices alone do
not provide sufficient detail for the interested reader. The descriptions of strategy, background, and personalities in the locker room
and boardroom provide important context for the quantitative data
on the adjacent pages of the paper. It is not unreasonable that we
provide at least the same balance of numerical and verbal description
when it comes to educational performance.

• **Provide data in a consistent format.** There is a broad mandate
that teachers and principals are to engage in "data-driven decision
making," and the data to which the phrase refers is frequently student performance on state tests. Teaching a generation of teachers
and principals to analyze test data—something that was never a part

of their university undergraduate or graduate school curricula—is difficult enough under perfect circumstances. This challenge is compounded when the state provides three different tests—perhaps one for reading, another for writing, and yet another for mathematics—and all three use different terminology and measurements to describe student proficiency. One performance assessment uses a seven-point rubric, while another one uses a four-point rubric. Thus a "3" is not proficient on one test, but is proficient on another. Each test has a different vendor providing test data in a different format, making it difficult or impossible for a teacher to create a comprehensive record of the performance of a single student. Only a few states are using unique student identifiers so that teachers can follow the progress of the same student from one year to the next. The norm—not the exception—is the spectacle of teachers and principals performing hand calculations and constructing handmade charts of student performance in order to analyze the data that they need. Such primitive and time-consuming analytical techniques are, to put it mildly, incongruous in an environment where hundreds of millions of dollars are devoted to state testing contracts. For the future, state policymakers should demand that vendors collaborate with one another in order to provide a single range of scores and a single set of terminology to describe student proficiency. Moreover, vendors should provide data to schools in a form that can be easily used on the computer on the teacher's desk. The software required should be no more complicated than the spreadsheet programs that are already in virtually every school. In brief, the ultimate "customers" for the vendors of state test data are not only state department and legislative officials, but also teachers who must use the data to plan improved instructional strategies and improve student achievement.

• **Balance an emphasis on compliance with the identification of best practices.** Most state departments of education have a legal responsibility to ensure compliance with legislative mandates. Moreover, a significant degree of the responsibility for compliance with federal programs has been shifted to states in the past several years. Thus it is only natural that state departments of education focus on compliance, and school systems are likely to view the state department as a source of rule enforcement more than a resource for best practices. There are, however, exceptional examples of state departments that provide a gold mine of best practices and that are relentlessly constructive in their approach to school improvement. The mention of any noteworthy examples risks the criticism that some excellent state departments of education have been omitted. Thus while the reader would find a great deal to commend in the Web sites of the state departments of California, Florida, Illinois, Massachusetts, Texas, Virginia, and Wisconsin, there are doubtless other state departments that have also balanced an emphasis on compliance with a search for best practices.

• **Make standards and assessment documents readable.** Here is an interesting challenge for the governor, senior education official, or state board member for any state. Select a sate academic standard at random—any grade, any subject—and ask yourself if you could use that exact language to communicate with children and their parents what is necessary for school success. Select an assessment document—the very ones that new teachers with a four-year undergraduate degree are routinely required to use to draw important inferences about student achievement and teaching strategies—and ask if your own educational background would equip you to understand and apply those statistics. A few states have risen to this challenge, making a point of expressing their standards and assessments in plain English. In many cases, however, the policymaker will see evidence of jargon, complexity, and ambiguity forming an impenetrable mess of words and numbers. One of the great gifts that state policymakers bring to the table is a deliberate naiveté—their willingness to ask the questions that are too infrequently posed, lest the questioner's sophistication be called into question. Yet when it comes to the constructive use of educational accountability, the illusion of sophistication is no virtue, and the willing appearance of simplicity is no vice.

• **Set the tone for civil discourse.** Among the most important contributions that state policymakers can make to educational issues is the manner in which the public debate is conducted. State officials are, by nature, political. I do not employ the term "political" with a sneer and negative connotation, but rather with the precise meaning of the term. The political process is one in which broad and diverse constituencies are heard and elected officials form a reasoned judgment based on the greater good. These judgments are never universally popular, but the process by which they are formed can be one that engenders respect and civic involvement, or one that creates distrust and disengagement. In policy matters involving children and jobs, feelings are strong and tensions run high. The tone of the debate over educational policy, however, is unproductive when the thoughtful contemplation of policy alternatives is replaced with a series of angry epithets and challenges to the motives of the opposition. In *The Leader's Guide to Standards* (Reeves, 2002c), I suggested the following considerations for state officials and every person who advocates a policy position before state policymakers. First, is the presentation related to our primary mission of improving student achievement for all children in the state? It is not sufficient that the idea has merit or that one feels strongly about it or that it influences the opportunities for the students in one neighborhood, community, or family. It must be related to the primary educational mission of the state. Second, is the presentation supported by evidence that can be independently verified? The phrases "research proves" and "studies show" must be associated with detailed evidence and citations. The standard should be the "preponderance of the evidence," rather than a set of dueling rhetoricians, each of whom has an article, anecdote, study, or glib assertion to support a point of view. Third, can the advocate answer thoughtful questions from the other side or merely parrot a prepared speech? And finally, can the advocate respond to challenges with thoughtful answers in an environment of civility and respect? The competing forces working on state legislators and educational policymakers inevitably yield compromises that provide full satisfaction to no one. Nevertheless, these policies can be forged in an atmosphere that give our citizens and children reason to be proud of the political system, to understand and respect well-reasoned differences of opinion, and most important, to remain engaged in the process for years to come.

7

Putting It All Together: Standards, Assessment, and Accountability

Although the focus of this book is accountability, we cannot complete our consideration of the topic without a discussion of the context in which accountability typically occurs—academic standards and student assessments. In the past decade, the use of academic standards has grown from being the foundation for educational reform in about a dozen states to being the foundation of curriculum and assessment in all 50 states. Before that time, most developed countries had already established national academic standards, and many of them incorporated a national standards-based curriculum as well. Despite the prevalence of standards, however, considerable controversy remains over the degree to which standards should be implemented (Reeves 2003a, 2003b; Reeves & Brandt, 2003) and whether standards fundamentally deprive schools of local control and teachers of academic freedom (Ohanian, 1999). My purpose here is not to rehash all of the elements of that debate, but rather to make the essential link between the constructive form of educational accountability advocated in these pages and the use of standards, rather than the bell curve, as the proper way to evaluate student performance. Finally, I consider the effect that standards and constructive accountability have on classroom assessment. Although discussions of educational accountability inevitably focus on external assessments, the continuing theme of this book has been that the judgment of the classroom teacher is an integral part of constructive accountability. One of the "big lies" of educational accountability systems is that the increasing use of standardized tests by state departments of education renders the assessment capability of the classroom teacher irrelevant. In fact, assessment literacy (Stiggins, 2001) has taken on a striking new importance. Only when accountability, standards, and assessment are fully integrated at the classroom level will we achieve the potential for fairness, equity of opportunity, and improved academic achievement that teaching professionals crave and society demands.

Why Standards?

Winston Churchill said of the democratic form of government that it was the worst of all systems—except for all the others. So it is with academic standards. They are too numerous (Marzano, 2003) and sometimes inappropriate for the grade level (Reeves & Brandt, 2003). Moreover, the language of standards varies widely from state to state, with words such as "indicators," "objectives," "benchmarks," and "standards" all referring to what students should know and be able to do (Reeves, 2002c). As a result, the basic case for standards has been lost in the chaos, jargon, and inarticulate expressions of educational policymakers and theorists. Before any constructive discussion of standards can ensue, we must bring order from chaos, confess the errors of the past, and make the essential case for standards.

Standards or the Bell Curve?

There are only two ways to evaluate student performance. We can compare the performance of a student to another student or to the average of a group of students, or we can compare the performance of the student to an objective standard. When we take the former approach, we have accepted the logic of the "normal distribution," or the bell curve. We care not whether a student has achieved a result, but only whether the student being evaluated is better or worse than his colleagues. In some instances such a comparative process makes sense. For example, we can assert that the World Series must produce only one winner, selected from two cities in Canada and two and a half dozen areas of the United States. Only one country can win the America's Cup, which at this writing is a contest between Switzerland and New Zealand. Only one country can win the World Cup of cricket, which consistently excludes the United States, China, and Russia. All of these contests share, in addition to their peculiarities of title and cultural exclusion, a commitment to determine excellence on a comparative basis. The arbiters of each sport care not who is a competent shortstop, batsman, or helmsman, but rather who beat whom. Victory connotes competence. Would this be the case if we changed the venue from the cricket match to the cockpit, from the ballpark to the driver's seat of an automobile? We gain scant comfort from the pilot who announces, "I'm proud to announce that my score on the aviation exam was better than my competitors, though I'm not quite sure how to land this airplane." We are unimpressed by the teenage driver who implores, "Give me a break, Dad—that dent isn't nearly as bad as the one Bobby put in his family's car!" In matters of safety, we compare pilots and teenage drivers not to one another, but to objective standards. We require equal numbers of take-offs and landings, and we insist that drivers adhere to the rules of the road. On matters that are deadly serious, we use standards. In matters of games, we use comparative measurements.

Standards—Nothing New

Standards are hardly new to education. In vocational and technical education, teachers place students in harm's way if they fail to have adequate safety standards. The student with nine fingers is not advanced over the student with eight fingers because the former was superior in a safety competition involving a buzz saw. The class has a standard of safety, and part of that standard is that students leave the class with the same number of fingers with which they entered. Kindergarten teachers do not expect students to know a few more letters of the alphabet than their competitors but to know every letter. With evaluation schemes that are precise and clear, they can tell parents and students which letters, colors, and shapes students know and thus provide clear guidance on what students must do in order to be prepared for the next level of learning. Music educators are quite confident about the difference between the A and the A-flat, with the former corresponding to about 440 cycles per second and readily identifiable from a standard tuning fork or electronic instrument. They never say, "Your performance of that note was better than any A we have heard today—go to the head of the class!" Rather, they can help the most and least advanced students to work, adjust, listen, and adjust again until they achieve the standard—hitting the A with precision.

Why, then, have standards become such a controversial subject, implemented with inconsistency and rancor? The best explanation is that the examples I have provided illustrate matters of easy consensus and clear differentiation between the attainment of a standard and the failure to meet it. But if the context is changed from safety to Sartre, from kindergarten to Kierkegaard, from music to Malthus, then objectivity is supplanted by subjectivity. In matters of literature, philosophy, or social science, the argument goes, proficiency is no longer clear, and the definition of acceptable student performance must rest with the judgment of experts. This logic is appealing, particularly to the experts whose judgments remain secure in direct proportion to their mystery. If students do not know how a judgment is made but have faith in the judge, the infallibility is ensured. Call it the "Oz effect." The great and powerful Oz retains power as long as there is no Dorothy and Toto to look behind the curtain. But, as Frank Baum reminds us, the distance from Oz to humbug is short indeed. So it is with academic performance in any subject. The injection of mystery into the description of student proficiency is less a function of complexity than difficulty. It is hard to describe what a student must do to be successful, and that is part of what makes the profession of teaching such a complex enterprise. It is particularly hard to differentiate the student who is progressing but not yet proficient from the student who is proficient, and the student who is proficient from the one who is exemplary. But that is what teachers must do every minute of the day.

Characteristics of Standards-Based Evaluation

The differences between standards-based evaluation and evaluation based on the bell curve are profound. These differences lie at the heart of the application of standards and, as a result, the implementation of an accountability system that is fair. Accountability for learning is not a matter of who beat whom, but rather an inquiry into which students, schools, teachers, and leaders have met the standards that lead to excellence and equity. If you are uncertain as to which choice—standards or the bell curve—your accountability system has made, the following contrasts should make the alternatives clear.

Standards are fixed; norms move. There is no 50th percentile when it comes to applying the Pythagorean theorem. The square of the hypotenuse is equal to the sum of the squares of the two sides, period. My students need not be merely a little bit better than their geometrically challenged peers; they must understand and apply the theorem at hand. For every area of student achievement, whether it involves using safe procedures in the science lab, turning in projects on time for a senior thesis in high school, or calculating sums in the 2nd grade, teachers can establish fixed standards of achievement that do not change. Student performance moves toward a goal that is clear and immutable. If the goal is to beat other children (particularly if that group consists of an anonymous sample used by a testing company to represent the national norm), then standards are murky and elusive. We never know during the performance, or even immediately after it, if we have achieved the objective. Only after our work has been compared to that of others do we know if it is acceptable. In a standards-based environment, by contrast, students, teachers, and parents know immediately when success has been achieved. If success has not been achieved, then we need not wait for an external judgment to be rendered, but can immediately determine the difference between the student's performance and the expected standard, provide timely feedback, and within minutes give the student additional opportunities to achieve success. The bell curve is about announcing who is not successful; standards allow every student to move toward success because the definition of that benchmark is clear and transparent.

Standards are cooperative; norms are competitive. When I ask employers what skills they expect of students in the 21st century, they rarely provide a list of facts to be stored and recalled. Rather, they almost always insist that their future employees have good work habits and the ability to work in a team environment. Such a cooperative spirit can be either nurtured or diminished in school, and the choice between the bell curve and standards provides such a stark opportunity. When students learn that they need not be proficient but only be better than their peers, cooperation evaporates. Everyone can fail to achieve the intended result of a science experiment, but if Sarah's graph is a bit more tidy than Elaine's, then Sarah will presumably have the edge in points, if not in proficiency. This scene is played out every night around dinner tables when students protest that, although their work is not what the teacher expected, it is "better than the other kids'." With such justifications, we pave the road to mediocrity. When proficiency is achieved in such an environment, proficient students have an active disincentive to help their colleagues who are still working toward proficiency.

This is in stark contrast to those schools reviewed in Chapter 5, where even the most casual observers can see cooperative spirit. Although individual achievement is respected and celebrated, no victory is complete until all students in a group have achieved the goal. The ubiquitous tables and graphs around these schools speak to the goal of proficiency for all students. The trophy case is not restricted to displays of the achievements of individuals or small groups, but to displays that show progress toward 100 percent of students achieving an objective. Goleman (1998) and Goleman, Boyatzis, and McKee (2002) have demonstrated conclusively that the emotional intelligence of students—the ability to empathize, to exercise self-control, to work collaboratively—is a far greater contributor to the subsequent workplace success of individuals than is their IQ or other measures of analytical intelligence. Of course, academic work and traditional intelligence are important concepts; they are necessary requirements for competence in the workplace, but are insufficient for complete workplace success. Standards promote emotional intelligence because they require that students not only understand complex information for their own needs, but also that they empathize with colleagues who are experiencing difficulty in mastering the material. This consistent commitment to mutual assistance, alternative teaching techniques, empathy, and group mastery is precisely what the world's most sophisticated technological enterprises need—and what schools can provide if we base the achievement of success on standards rather than on a competition that yields nonproficient winners and—just as bad for long-term motivation—proficient losers.

Standards are challenging; norms are dumbed-down. In the early days of the standards debate, it was an article of faith by the advocates of the bell curve that comparison yielded rigor. Any class, the argument went, in which all students could achieve an *A* was evidence of grade inflation and low standards. Classes with no *A*s and too many low grades faced a public relations problem. Thus the "normal" distribution of grades, with a few high grades, a few low grades, and most grades in the middle, became a self-fulfilling prophecy. As more schools have become committed to standards, however, the assertions supporting the equivalence between the bell curve and rigor can be tested. As we have seen in case after case of high-poverty schools that have achieved success under a standards-based environment, the commitment of educators to move away from accepting low grades as a part of the sociological landscape has been accompanied by strikingly high expectations. When they say (and mean), "Failure is not an option," these teachers and students are engaging in more than sloganeering. They are explicitly rejecting the bell curve and embracing a standard that all students can and must achieve. Far from lowering their standards, these schools achieve excellence that is on a par with or, in the cases cited earlier, beyond the present performance of their economically advanced peers.

As critics bemoan the "dumbing down" of the school curriculum, their rhetorical arrows should be aimed in the right direction—not at teachers, but at a system that validates performance that is wretched but "good enough compared to other kids'." When some school systems explicitly set lower standards for schools in high-poverty areas than those in low-poverty areas (Goodnough & Medina, 2003), they are explicitly saying that their standards are not consistent. Worse yet, they are saying that their standards will be lower for students in poverty. Imagine the public outcry if a local health department announced that restaurant hygiene standards would be reduced for establishments in high-poverty areas because "everyone knows that workers in poor restaurants cannot be expected to have achievement as high as that in wealthy neighborhoods." The charges of racism and classism would lead to justified public outrage. Using the same logic, however, to justify different standards for poor schools than for wealthy schools is cause for celebration in some quarters. The *New York Times* (Goodnough & Medina, 2003) quoted a self-described "advocate for children" as saying, "There is an understanding nationally that you can't compare apples with oranges. You can't compare a school with kids from Scarsdale with kids starting from Bushwick. It's really that simple."

Such an argument plays well in the fact-free environment that surrounds many educational debates, but the stakes are too high to let such a preposterous assertion pass without challenge. First, we can cite abundant evidence of successful student achievement in schools with large numbers of poor and minority students. Robert Marzano's recent meta-analysis synthesizing 35 years of research on the subject (2003) makes clear that factors inside the school, including time, curriculum, feedback, and frequent assessment, have a greater effect on student achievement than do demographic characteristics. My own research of high-poverty, high-minority, high-performing schools is another pebble on this mountain of research. What makes these success stories rare is not the inability of poor and minority children, but the unwillingness of policymakers to maintain the same expectations for poor kids as they do for those who are economically advantaged.

Classroom Assessment: The Essential Link

As I was finishing the final sentences of this chapter, I received a call from a district whose superintendent had been remarkably successful in her previous district in improving student achievement and equity. One of the most important techniques she used was the administration of common assessments, collaboratively scored, at every grade level. Every month students, parents, teachers, and administrators knew how students were performing on their most important standards. They knew that the state test was too late to matter to many students and that the feedback from the state test was insufficient to influence teaching and learning in a meaningful way. Moreover, these terrific teachers had a story to tell and had student achievements worthy of celebration every month. Finally, the monthly data allowed colleagues to learn from each other as they observed one another's successes and emulated the best practices of their colleagues. Despite this history of success, the challenges were unremitting:

"If teachers publish the results of monthly assessments, they might be compared to one another, and this would be humiliating." (Never mind that the purpose of such a comparison is a search for successful practices, not a search for humiliation.)

"If the data are published, teachers will fear being fired." (Never mind that the district was willing to stipulate that no job action would ever be taken based on a single assessment of student results.)

"There is too much pressure on students and teachers to perform now, and this will just increase the pressure." (Never mind that the pressure on students and teachers from external state tests remains unremitting, and the use of locally scored common assessments allows students and teachers to celebrate regular progress and, where performance is low, to quickly recover rather than wait for an entire year for validation.)

The evidence from holistic accountability systems is clear: classroom assessment, created and scored by classroom teachers, is the gold standard in educational accountability. One would think that teachers would embrace this philosophy, because it honors them as professionals and places their efforts on a par with the authors of nationally prominent tests that normally garner all the public attention. Amazingly, however, some of the fiercest resistance to teacher-created tests comes not from the defenders of national testing companies but from the classroom teachers themselves.

We are at a crossroads in educational accountability, and neither fork in the road leads backward to an era of minimal accountability without public scrutiny. One fork in the road—that taken by the vast majority of schools in the early years of the 21st century—is the road toward externally driven accountability. Teachers in this model are cogs in the wheel, doing their best to prepare students for externally generated tests. Their value is determined by the performance of students on those tests; the teachers' actions in the classroom, their design of curriculum, and the decisions of their leaders are all irrelevant. "Just give us the results," scream the signs on this fork in the road. If the context were a campaign for weight loss, this path would not care if the patients lose weight as a result of diet and exercise or as a result of anorexia and drug abuse—as long as the resulting weight loss hits the target, this philosophy of accountability is well satisfied.

The other fork in the road offers a more challenging and far more rewarding approach. Although accountability will certainly include external tests, systems that are comprehensive, holistic, and constructive will focus on student assessment at the classroom level. These classroom assessments will not be secretive, but will be transparently linked to state academic standards. Every student will have the opportunity for success, rigor, and challenge. Because feedback will be immediate and specific, these assessments will be used to improve teaching and learning, not merely to evaluate students and schools. The creation of an accountability system without significant care and attention to classroom assessment, data analysis, and subsequent improvements in teaching, curriculum, and leadership will be little more than one more public relations nightmare for our public schools. True accountability for learning, by contrast, will strike the balanced middle ground among the warring factions in today's educational policy debates. Because of the emphasis on measurement of learning and the inclusion of external measurements, the advocates of strong accountability, public reporting, and external standards will be recognized. Because of the emphasis on classroom assessment and the respect for teacher creativity and judgment, the advocates of teacher-led accountability will be recognized.

Recognition of these advocates, however, does not imply satisfaction. Public school critics will continue to ignore classroom and building evidence, focusing exclusively on average test scores from norm-referenced tests. They will regularly publish the unsurprising result that 49.9 percent of students are below average. Critics of accountability will continue to rail against any external testing, believing that teachers alone should govern the curriculum and assessment within the four walls of their classrooms.

Neither side in the continuing debate will be satisfied by the comprehensive approach of this book. But the choice before us is not the victory or defeat of one extreme or another. Rather, we must examine the evidence, consider the overriding needs of the students we serve, and make our best judgment. Holistic accountability, properly implemented, is not a destination but a journey. Whatever the test scores say, whatever the demographic characteristics of the students, whatever the prevailing direction of the political winds, holistic accountability provides respect for the decision making of teachers and school leaders. Almost certainly, some of the techniques suggested in this book will not work for you or for other colleagues in your school. Holistic accountability provides not perfection, but a systematic examination of teaching practices, curriculum, and leadership decisions. This examination leads to the recognition of success, the recognition of error, and the continuous improvement of teaching and learning.

Appendix A

A Sample Comprehensive Accountability System*

Table of Contents

---

*This example represents a synthesis of the actual accountability systems now in use in many school systems. I am particularly indebted to the leadership of the Norfolk Public Schools for the broad adaptation of their accountability model. Special thanks to Superintendent Dr. John Simpson; the present and immediate past presidents of the board of education, Dr. Theresa Whibley and Mrs. Anita Poston; and Deputy Superintendents Dr. Thomas Lockamy and Dr. Denise Schnitzer. Although this example may offer some useful ideas, each school system must develop its own accountability system based on its local requirements, state department of education requirements, and prevailing federal mandates.

1.0 Executive Summary

The purpose of the comprehensive accountability system is to improve student achievement, professional teaching practice, and leadership decision making within the school system. Although this system is bound by the requirements of state and federal law, the district has made a conscious decision to create an accountability system that is constructive, that is consistent with our mission and values, and that goes far beyond the minimum requirements of state and federal mandates. The system includes three levels of information:

Tier 1: Systemwide Indicators. These are the data points required by federal statute, state regulations, and local board of education policy. These indicators apply to every school in the district and include items such as state test scores, safety, attendance, dropout rates, and student performance grouped by demographic characteristics.

Tier 2: School-Based Indicators. These are the measurable practices in teaching, leadership, parent involvement, extracurricular activities, and other school-based indicators that reflect the decisions of the teachers, parents, and administrators in each school. Although each school has many programs and initiatives, these five indicators represent those measurable practices that are most important to each school leadership team.

Tier 3: School Narrative. Each school in the system will provide a one-page narrative that explains the connections between Tier 1 and Tier 2 indicators for that school and also explains factors in the school environment that were not amenable to quantitative measurement.

The district comprehensive accountability system is a result of the work of the Accountability Task Force, a group commissioned by the board of education and the superintendent of schools. The Task Force consisted of 18 members and included parents, business and community leaders, teachers, administrators, and a student representative. The Task Force presented its recommendations to the superintendent, who recommended adoption of this plan to the board of education. Although the original job of the Task Force was to create the comprehensive accountability plan, the superintendent has requested that the Task Force continue to meet quarterly in order to monitor the implementation of the accountability plan and to make recommendations for improvements in the plan to the superintendent.

The comprehensive accountability system supports the goals of the board of education, including student achievement, safe and secure schools, and community engagement. However, the manner in which these goals are met and the indicators that are chosen to reflect school-based strategies will vary widely from one school to another. Thus the comprehensive accountability system does not provide a "one size fits all" approach to education, but rather requires each school to determine the practices and programs that best meet the needs of its students. Because the results of Tiers 1, 2, and 3 will be published each year, school leadership teams throughout the system will have the opportunity to observe which Tier 2 practices have been most effective in achieving board goals and will have the opportunity to make adjustments in their Tier 2 indicators every year. Moreover, the superintendent and the board of education will have the opportunity to evaluate the extent to which each school is using available data from the comprehensive accountability system to achieve its improvement goals.

2.0 Accountability System Structure

2.1 The Accountability Task Force

The primary responsibility for developing the comprehensive accountability system lies with the Accountability Task Force. This group, appointed by the superintendent and confirmed by the board of education, represents a broad group of stakeholders in our community. Of 24 people invited to become members of the Task Force, 18 accepted and all of those members attended at least five of the seven meetings of the Task Force. Decisions on the structure of the comprehensive accountability system were reached by consensus, and the Task Force members unanimously supported this final report. Over the course of seven meetings from October through April, the Task Force examined the previous school improvement planning process, gathered information from local, regional, and national experts, and formulated the comprehensive accountability system represented by this document.

2.2 Changes from the School Improvement Planning Model

The new comprehensive accountability plan differs from the previous school improvement planning model both in scope and focus. The new plan not only involves an attention to test scores, but also includes other measures of student achievement. By using multiple measures of achievement, students, teachers, administrators, parents, and the community all share responsibility for school performance. While this plan meets the requirements of state and federal law for the reporting of test scores, the comprehensive accountability plan places those test scores in context by reporting additional data that shed light on the causes for variations in student achievement. These variables include not only the previously reported differences in student demographic characteristics, but also the differences in teacher qualifications, educational practices, leadership decision making, and parent/community support in each school. In addition to these quantitative measurements, the plan includes a narrative for each school, providing insight into which professional practices have the greatest impact on student achievement. In addition, the school narratives will help the community understand the "story behind the numbers" that is an essential part of every school.

Two key questions that teachers and administrators asked during the course of the Task Force deliberations were the following:

> *(1) "Does the new accountability system mean more work for me?"*

In every school, the Task Force found extraordinary efforts of teachers, administrators, and parents that were never reported as part of the previous accountability system, which focused almost exclusively on test scores. Thus the new comprehensive accountability system should not require additional work, but should rather ensure that the work currently accomplished receives recognition and appropriate public exposure. There will be additional work for those few schools that have not been documenting their leadership and teaching practices nor measuring the extent to which their parent and community involvement has taken place. The Task Force is persuaded, however, that the benefits of public reporting of this information far outweigh the costs. Moreover, the limitation of the reporting of school-based indicators to only five measurements will actually result in fewer data points than most schools have reported on in the past under the previous school improvement model.

(2) "Who is held accountable?"

Under the previous system, educational accountability was something "done to" students, who were the only ones bearing the consequences of the plan. Although many teachers expressed the fear that accountability meant that they would be fired or disciplined for low test scores, that was not the case in the previous system, nor is it the case in the new system. Rather, the new comprehensive accountability system makes clear that teachers and administrators are required to be transparent in their decision making, sharing with district leadership and the public the strategies that they employ to achieve district goals and measuring the extent to which those strategies are implemented. Inherent in the term "comprehensive" is the idea that accountability is the responsibility of all the stakeholders in the school district. This definition includes students, parents, teachers, administrators, other district employees, as well as businesses, nonprofit organizations, governmental offices, and other community members. Education is a community enterprise; every member of the community benefits from the success of this school system, and every community member suffers a cost when our education system fails to live up to its obligations. Thus the new comprehensive accountability system will include indicators on every central office department, as well as the degree to which community services have supported students and the degree to which parents and other community partners are engaged in supporting students and schools.

2.3 Principles of Effective Accountability

The Task Force considered the experiences of other school systems in the development of their accountability systems* and developed

---

*The Task Force used, among other resources, *Accountability in Action: A Blueprint for Learning Organizations* (Reeves, 2000a), *Holistic Accountability: Serving Students, Schools, and Community* (Reeves, 2002b), and Video Journal of Education, Volume 1001, *Accountability for Greater Student Learning* (Reeves, 2001c).

seven principles to guide the work of the Task Force. These seven principles, along with a key question, follow:

Congruence: Is the accountability system compatible with rewards and incentives already in place in the district?

Respect for diversity: Does the accountability system include multiple measures of student achievement, some of which apply to all schools and some of which apply to individual schools based on school needs?

Accuracy: Are the measures outlined for the system correct, are they used appropriately, and do they reflect the use of alternative evidence rather than only test scores?

Specificity: Does the accountability system delineate clear ideas of what is expected and what must be done to help students achieve (descriptive and prescriptive)?

Feedback for continuous improvement: Does the accountability system allow for both formative and summative evaluations, and are the results used to make informed decisions about school improvement and new initiatives?

Universality: Is there accountability not only for students, but also for central office, board members, parents, teachers, and school administrators?

Fairness: Is the accountability system structured so that everyone knows the rules of the game, the rules are applied consistently, and all have the opportunity to play by the same rules?

2.4 Accountability System Architecture

The architecture of the comprehensive accountability system provides three vantage points from which to gauge progress toward meeting the written school board goals and district objectives. For the purpose of the accountability system, these views are called "tiers" and consist of the following:

Tier 1: Tier 1 indicators are typically required by the state or the district and are used to determine the degree to which state and district expectations are being met. Tier 1 indicators are uniform for all schools of similar types, with every elementary school having identical Tier 1 indicators and each middle and high school also having indicators that are appropriate for those grade levels.

Tier 2: Tier 2 indicators are school based and are designed to help all schools continuously improve to meet state and district expectations. Tier 2 indicators are a reflection of the specific priorities of each school, and they may vary widely from one school to another. Whereas some schools may wish to use Tier 2 indicators to reflect their measurements of school-based writing programs, other schools will use Tier 2 indicators to reflect their unique programs of parent involvement, community engagement, student extracurricular activities, behavior and discipline programs, technology integration, or other combinations of academic and support programs.

Tier 3: Tier 3 is the qualitative portion of the system and provides a narrative description of the district and school efforts toward continuous improvement. Each Tier 3 narrative addresses two questions. First, "How does the information from Tier 1 and Tier 2 fit together?" The school selected specific Tier 2 indicators in the belief that these activities would improve Tier 1 measurements, and the narrative will explain the extent to which those expectations were met. Second, "What are the variables in the school that cannot be described numerically?" This gives each school the opportunity to describe the triumphs and tragedies of the students, staff, and surrounding community, along with a rich description of the cultural and organizational environment of the school.

2.5 Accountability System Reporting

In addition to these three tiers, the accountability system includes a plan for the reporting of district, departmental, and school performance, a district professional development plan on the accountability system, a dissemination of information plan, and an anticipated timeline for implementation of the comprehensive accountability system.

2.6 State and District Expectations

The state legislature and state department of education have established academic standards that form the basis of state requirements in curriculum, assessment, and accountability for student achievement. The state academic standards establish expectations for teaching and learning. These expectations are linked to state assessments that now include testing in reading and mathematics in grades 3 through 8, as well as a high school graduation assessment that is initially administered at the beginning of the 10th grade. These test results, along with data on student attendance and school safety, form the basis of the state-mandated school performance report card. Our district will comply with this state requirement, but we intend to supplement every report card with a report from the new comprehensive accountability system so that every parent understands not only what the state test results indicate, but also the many other important activities within the school. For example, while parents of high school students certainly want to know about the pass rate on the high school graduation exam, they will also want to know about student performance in Advanced Placement classes, student participation in extracurricular activities, and other important accountability indicators that are not included in the state report card.

3.0 Tier 1: Systemwide Indicators

3.1 Introduction

Several Tier 1 indicators monitor student academic achievement in every school based on uniform state and district requirements. These indicators are of special interest to the board of education, the state department of education, and the media. The state sets expectations for teaching and for learning through the state academic standards. The core standards clarify what students are expected to know and accomplish in English, math, science, history and social science, and computer technology. Student learning is measured by the state tests administered in elementary, middle, and high school, as well as district tests in writing. These tests measure content knowledge, scientific and mathematical processes, reading comprehension, vocabulary, writing, and reasoning abilities.

3.2 State Test Scores

The first Tier 1 indicator involves student performance on the state tests in the core subject areas. These tests provide a perspective of how students are meeting state standards and how they perform when compared with other students throughout the state. The second source of Tier 1 data will monitor the percentage of high school graduates taking the SAT I and ACT exams as well as the average composite scores on these exams. Both the SAT and the ACT give indications of the success of students in high school and also serve as a basis for comparisons of our high school students to their peers throughout the nation.

3.3 Equity and Curriculum Indicators

Another source of Tier 1 data is reflected on the state report card and is based on the percentages and diversity of students taking higher-level courses and the passing rates of those students enrolled in these courses. This indicator helps monitor the rigor of the academic offerings in our schools. The advanced academic programs monitored here include Advanced Placement, Dual Enrollment (that is, students receive both high school and college credit simultaneously for the same class), and International Baccalaureate classes. An additional Tier 1 indicator in the student achievement arena concerns the percentage of students reading at or above grade level from grades 3 through 8. Data from the Gates-MacGinitie Reading Tests are used to monitor academic achievement in this area. Other Tier 1 indicators include the average daily attendance rate of students, the percentage of students who drop out of school, the graduation rate, and the percent of teachers meeting state licensure requirements for grades or subjects that they teach.

3.4 Safe and Secure Learning Environment

In addition to the district's primary goal of improved student achievement, the district is committed to ensuring a safe, secure, and disciplined teaching and learning environment in schools. Several Tier 1 indicators will be used to meet this expectation. The sources of data for these indicators include monitoring the responses by students, teachers, and parents on the annual district Quality Schools Initiative climate survey. The state report card also includes school safety information such as the indicators of the number of incidents of physical violence, possession of firearms, and possession of other weapons. To get a more realistic picture of safety in the schools, three other district Tier 1 indicators are included. These indicators identify the percentage of students in each school WITHOUT incidents of physical violence, possession of firearms, and possession of weapons other than firearms. The reason that these Tier 1 statistics are important is that when the number of instances of disciplinary violations are counted, the same student can account for multiple violations. When the public sees the percentages of students who are not involved in any disciplinary violations, a more accurate portrayal of the safety of the school and the organizational climate can be provided.

3.5 Community Engagement

The last expectation at the district level revolves around the active engagement of parents, community members, and businesses in the educational process. Specifically, the districtwide Tier 1 indicators measure the frequency of opportunities for all involved parties to become engaged with the school. These opportunities include informal verbal communications, face-to-face meetings, and written communications (such as newsletters, informal notes, and personal letters), as well as Internet communications including e-mail and school Web site interactions. Other Tier 1 indicators under this area focus on the number of direct, interactive contacts involving student achievement that teachers and other staff members make with parents and/or guardians, the number of opportunities for parents and community members to assist in improving reading and mathematics proficiency, and the number of opportunities for various stakeholders to become ambassadors for the school district.

3.6 Additional Tier 1 Indicators

Several Tier 1 indicators are neither located on the State Report Card nor listed under the school board goals. However, these indicators reflect data required to be reported at the state and/or district levels. These indicators include Stanford 9 test results, promotion/retention statistics, the percentage of students missing 10 or more days of school, PSAT results, and the percentage of students who graduate after four to six years of high school and who have been enrolled in the district all of these years. Several other Tier 1 indicators not included on the State Report Card nor explicitly stated in the district objectives include information about teachers teaching in their specific areas of endorsement. Indicators in this area include the percentage of classes taught by teachers endorsed for those classes and the percent of special education and gifted education positions occupied by teachers with endorsements in special education and gifted education respectively. Another Tier 1 indicator identifies the number of professional development hours related to academic achievement that are offered to and attended by staff members.

3.7 Disaggregation of Data

To ensure our commitment to equity and transparency, data for several of these indicators will be disaggregated by ethnicity, primary language, and eligibility for free and reduced lunch. The Task Force strongly encourages the use of disaggregated data for policy analysis, not for the creation of interventions for students based solely on their demographic characteristics.

4.0 Tier 2: School-Based Indicators

4.1 Overview of Tier 2 Indicators

Each school will be held accountable for level-appropriate Tier 1 indicators as these all are monitored at the state and district level. In addition, each school will select seven indicators from the Tier 2 indicators listed in the appendices to this plan. The Task Force recognizes that unanticipated events may prevent the completion of some school-based initiatives or the complete and accurate recording of all data for Tier 2 indicators. Therefore, although each school will identify seven Tier 2 indicators, they will report on only five of those indicators at the end of each year. The selection of these five indicators is left to the discretion of the school leadership team.

4.2 Tier 2 Menu and Alternative Indicator Selections

Tier 2 indicators reflect the teaching strategies used to help meet Tier 1 indicators. The Tier 2 indicators listed in the appendix to this document are measurable and directly relate to the support of Tier 1 indicators. Schools may include Tier 2 indicators not on this menu if they have a reasonable basis for believing that specific measurable practices for their school-based indicator will be related to the achievement of one or more Tier 1 indicators.

4.3 Data Collection and Monitoring for Tier 2 Indicators

The school leadership team will determine the school-level indicators based on a careful analysis of current data, programs, needs, and goals. These indicators become a part of the school accountability report and the planning documents that support this plan. Data for the selected school-level indicators will be collected by the school and used to continuously monitor progress during the year. These self-selected indicators will be the only school-level indicators included in the annual school performance report. A list of the seven Tier 2 indicators selected by each school will be forwarded to the district accountability officer by October 1 of each school year, or, in the case of schools on alternative schedules, Tier 2 indicators will be submitted to the district accountability office within 30 calendar days after the beginning of the new school year. Each school will submit data on the performance of Tier 2 indicators to the district accountability office twice each year, on January 15 and June 15.

4.4 Accountability Task Force Monitoring

Because the primary purpose of the comprehensive accountability system is the improvement of teaching and learning, the data collected from Tier 2 indicators will be regularly reviewed and analyzed by the Task Force, and the results of that analysis will be shared with school leadership teams throughout the district. As a result of the sharing of these insights and best practices, schools will have the opportunity to make annual improvements in the selection of their Tier 2 indicators as well as the manner in which Tier 2 indicators are implemented and measured. In the course of a school year, schools may wish to modify or completely change some Tier 2 indicators. The Task Force will review and approve requests for changes so that schools can make appropriate midcourse corrections and not remain committed to Tier 2 indicators that are inappropriate or unhelpful for the students and faculty of that school. To gain maximum value from

Tier 2 indicators, schools must regularly monitor their performance and ask reflective questions such as the following:

- "Are we doing what we said we would do?"
- "Are we measuring our Tier 2 indicators consistently and accurately?"
- "How are our efforts in Tier 2 indicators related to observable changes in student achievement?"
- "If some of our Tier 2 indicators are not working satisfactorily, how can they be modified? If the indicator in question cannot be modified, what is a better Tier 2 indicator that we can use to replace it?"
- "If we have an unsatisfactory experience with a Tier 2 indicator, what have we learned from that, and how will this experience inform our future professional practices and leadership decision-making processes?"

Although these deliberations are not required reports, the minutes of these meetings will reflect the extent to which the school leadership team is using data constructively to address the priorities and challenges of the school.

4.5 Changes in Tier 2 Indicators

Each year, school leadership teams will conduct an internal evaluation of Tier 2 indicators by evaluating how Tier 2 indicators used by that school and by other schools throughout the district are related (or not related) to Tier 1 objectives in student achievement, safety, and community engagement. Each year, schools will have the opportunity to confirm their existing Tier 2 indicators or they may select new Tier 2 indicators.

5.0 Tier 3: School Narratives

5.1 Introduction

Tier 3 allows each school to address two critical questions. First, what inferences does the school leadership team draw between its performance on Tier 2 indicators, reflecting its chosen school-based strategies, and the school's performance on Tier 1 indicators, reflecting the priorities of state and district policymakers? Second, what are the factors in the school climate that help to place quantitative data in context? This allows the school to explain the triumphs and tragedies that had a profound impact on the students, faculty, and community but that are not readily apparent from an examination of the data on test scores, attendance, and graduation rates.

5.2 Format and Content of the School Narrative

This school narrative must be no more than 600 words and should be written in language that is accessible to parents and community members. The narrative is an ideal opportunity for the school to highlight programs that are not reflected in Tier 1 or Tier 2. For example, the school narrative can provide details on the extracurricular activities, music, art, and physical education programs; parent and community engagement programs; and the professional development activities of the faculty. In sum, the school narrative is "the story behind the numbers" and will help members of the Task Force assess and recommend specific strategies for school improvement throughout the district.

6.0 Professional Development Plan

6.1 Introduction

Teachers, school-level administrators, and central office administrators were introduced to the philosophy and concepts underlying the comprehensive accountability system during the last academic year. Specifically, every faculty member and administrator has received an orientation to the comprehensive accountability system and a full-day practical exercise in data-driven decision making based on the real data for each school. For a more detailed explanation of the data-driven decision-making process, see Chapter 7 of *The Leader's Guide to Standards* (Reeves, 2002c).

6.2 School-Based Professional Development

Once each school used the data-driven decision-making process to identify its priorities and Tier 2 indicators, then subsequent professional development decisions were based on those identified needs. For example, schools that chose writing as an emphasis have used the "Writing Excellence" workshops and resources such as *Reason to Write* (Reeves, 2002e). Schools that focused on improving standards-based performance assessments have used the "Making Standards Work" seminars and resources such as *Power Standards, Unwrapping the Standards,* and *Making Standards Work* (Reeves, 2003b). Other schools have focused on differentiated instruction, parent involvement, technology integration, academic enrichment, reading fundamentals, or other strategies and have used a combination of internal and external resources to support the professional development that supports the comprehensive accountability plan.

6.3 Building Resources

To help teachers understand and use the comprehensive accountability system planned for the next school year, principals will facilitate school-based professional development sessions using the Video Journal of Education, Volume 1001, *Accountability for Greater Student Learning* (Reeves, 2001c). Time will also be dedicated at principal meetings for exchanging ideas on how to involve staff, parents, and community in implementing accountability for greater learning.

7.0 Communication Plan

7.1 Introduction

The purpose of the comprehensive accountability system is the improvement of learning and teaching throughout the school system. Therefore, it is essential that the results of the accountability system be communicated to stakeholders inside the system and throughout the community. The true test of the value of the accountability system lies in how the results are used to make constructive and meaningful decisions to improve teaching and learning. In addition to the annual report of the comprehensive accountability system, we will use periodic reports to the community to highlight the constructive use of accountability to improve teaching and learning. In addition to the use of principal meetings, the school system will use multiple means of communication, including the district intranet, local public access television, parent-teacher organization meetings, and other community briefings.

7.2 School Reports

The principal and the school leadership team share the responsibility for preparing the individual school portion of the accountability report. This report includes the performance of each school on the systemwide Tier 1 indicators, the school-based Tier 2 indicators, and the Tier 3 school narrative. The reason that these reports will be available to any interested person on the district's Web site is that the district is committed to the constructive use of accountability data to improve student achievement.

7.3 Community Report

The Task Force will be responsible for preparing an accountability report for the community. This report will include data on all Tier 1 indicators as well as an analysis of the Tier 2 indicators that had the most direct relationship to success on Tier 1 indicators. The purpose of the community report is not to rank or compare schools, but rather to share with the community the professional practices and leadership decisions that were most directly related to the priorities of the school system and the community.

7.4 State Report

The report to the state department of education is a matter of statutory compliance. This district is committed to the principle of "overcompliance" with state and federal mandates and therefore will report not only the requirements of the state and federal laws related to educational accountability, but will also report additional information from the district accountability system, such as Tier 2 and Tier 3 information, that is well beyond the requirements of state and federal mandates.

8.0 Central Office Accountability System

8.1 Introduction

This school system is committed to the belief that all staff members are held accountable for the goals and objectives of the district. Educational accountability is not something that is "done to" students and teachers but rather is a system of continuous improvement that involves every stakeholder, including students, teachers, parents, administrators, bus drivers, cafeteria workers, custodians, and central office administrators. Therefore, various departments within the central office (academic affairs, finance, information, and operations) also are a part of the comprehensive accountability system adopted by the district. The accountability system for the central office will provide a means by which personnel in departments can measure and monitor progress toward supporting the district objectives. The central office accountability system closely mirrors the architecture of the system used by the schools and the district. The three district objectives will serve as the common Tier 1 objectives for departments in the central office, and central office departments will be held accountable for Tier 1 indicators, either directly or indirectly. Therefore, all staff members will be working toward and supporting improved academic achievement; a safe, secure, and disciplined learning environment; and the involvement of external stakeholders in the educational process. These objectives will be shared by every department within the central office. As is the case with every school, each department will select seven Tier 2 indicators for yearly improvement, and the final accountability report will include five of these seven indicators. As is the case with schools, central office departments will create professional development plans that are linked to the accountability system indicators so that professional learning is explicitly linked to departmental performance.

8.2 Departmental Performance Report

Central office departments will complete a departmental performance report by July 15 of each year. The departmental performance report will include data for five of the seven targeted Tier 2 indicators, with the selection of the five Tier 2 indicators made by the department director. In addition, the department will submit a departmental narrative that parallels the Tier 3 narratives of the district and the schools. The departmental narrative will address connections between departmental strategies (Tier 2 indicators) and departmental results (Tier 1 indicators), as well as highlight the activities, organizational climate, and other features of departmental performance that may not be evident in the quantitative data from Tier 1 and Tier 2.

Appendix A-1: Accountability Task Force

District Administrators

Superintendent of Schools

Deputy Superintendent, Academic Affairs

Deputy Superintendent, Operations

Senior Coordinator, Compensatory Programs

Senior Director, Computing Technology

Senior Director, Compensatory Programs

Senior Director, Research, Testing, and Statistics

District Chief Financial Officer

Senior Director, Special and Gifted Education

Senior Coordinator, Communications Skills

Senior Director, Accounting

Senior Director, Staff Development and Human Relations

School Administrators

Elementary School Principal

Middle School Principal

High School Principal

Teachers

Elementary School Teacher

Middle School Teacher

High School Teacher

Alternative School Teacher

Parents

> Representative of the Elementary School Advisory Council
>
> Representative of the Middle School Advisory Council
>
> Representative of the High School Advisory Council
>
> Representative of the Special Education Advisory Council
>
> Representative of the Gifted Education Advisory Council

Appendix A-2: Tier 1 Indicators

1.0 Academic Achievement

1.1 Reporting Format

Each academic achievement indicator will be reported in the following manner:

> 1.1.1 Score for all students.
>
> 1.1.2 Score for regular education students.
>
> 1.1.3 Score for regular education students continuously enrolled since the second week of school.
>
> 1.1.4 Score for regular education students, continuously enrolled, with attendance rates of 90 percent or higher.

In addition, each report will include disaggregation by student eligibility for free and reduced lunch, ethnic identity, and English language status.

1.2 State Test Scores

Percentage of students identified as "proficient" or higher on all state and district tests.

1.3 College Admissions Scores (High School Only)

Percentage of students taking either the SAT or ACT, and average score for students on each test.

1.4 Advanced Placement (AP) Scores (High School Only)

Percentage of students taking AP classes, percentages of students in AP classes taking AP tests for each subject, and percentage of students scoring a "3" or higher on AP tests. Percentage of students taking International Baccalaureate (IB) classes, percentage of students in IB classes taking IB tests for the IB diploma, and percentage of students receiving IB credit for each test.

1.5 Reading Scores
Percentage of students scoring at or above grade level on the Gates MacGinitie Reading Tests.

2.0 Attendance
Average daily attendance rate, computed using the state's formula. In addition, each school will report the percentage of students with attendance rates of 90 percent or higher.

3.0 Persistence
Percentage of students who complete the year at that school or any other identifiable continuation of their education. (Note: The purpose of this indicator is to gain an accurate measurement of the dropout rate, excluding students who leave the school to participate in another educational program.)

4.0 Promotion
Percentage of students who are recommended for promotion to the next grade.

5.0 Teacher Qualifications
Percentage of classes (in the secondary level, percentage of courses) taught by teachers who have subject matter and grade-level certification. Percentage of special education students who receive instruction from teachers with special education certification.

6.0 Professional Development
Number and percentage of professional development hours that are directly related to the school's Tier 1 or Tier 2 accountability indicators.

7.0 Safety
Percentage of students not involved in disciplinary incidents. Percentage of students not involved in violent disciplinary incidents (assaults, fights, or weapons possession). Number of disciplinary incidents. Number of violent disciplinary incidents.

Appendix A-3: Tier 2 Indicators

Note: The following menu of Tier 2 indicators is suggestive only. Schools choose seven Tier 2 indicators based on their unique needs and report five of those seven indicators for the year-end accountability report. Schools may create additional Tier 2 indicators, with the review and approval of the Accountability Task Force. Ideally, measurement of Tier 2 indicators should be taken throughout the year so that the faculty and staff can review the data, make midcourse corrections, and continuously improve teaching and learning.

- Percentage of students who score "proficient" or higher on school-based criterion-referenced reading assessments.

- Percentage of students who score "proficient" or higher on standards-based performance assessments in _____ (specify subject).

- Percentage of students scoring "proficient" or higher on school-based writing assessments.

- Number of writing assessments scored collaboratively by two or more teachers.

- Percentage of _____ (specify subject) assessments requiring student writing.

- Percentage of _____ (specify subject) assessments requiring student oral presentations.

- Percentage of students scoring "proficient" or higher on a school-based public speaking rubric.

- Percentage of students scoring "proficient" or higher on school-based math problem-solving assessments.

- Percentage of students scoring "proficient" or higher on school-based social studies assessments.

- Percentage of students scoring "proficient" or higher on school-based science assessments.

- Percentage of assessments in _____ (specify subject) requiring student application of computer technology.

- Number of learning activities that explicitly involve community or business partnerships.

- Percentage of special area assessments (music, art, physical education, world language, technology) that explicitly include academic standards in language arts, math, science, or social studies.

- Percentage of students who are "proficient" or better using two-column note taking based on a school-based note-taking rubric.

- Percentage of students who are "proficient" or better using an assignment planning notebook and calendar based on a school-based rubric.

- Percentage of students involved in extracurricular activities.

- Percentage of students completing individualized learning plan objectives.

- Percentage of teachers completing individualized learning plan objectives.

- Percentage of students involved in nine or more hours of community service.

- Percentage of students with parent or significant adult involved in nine or more hours of school volunteer work.

- Percentage of students participating in visual or performing arts.

- Percentage of students scoring "proficient" or higher on a grade-appropriate research project.

- Percentage of students completing personal Web pages posted on the school Web site or intranet.

Appendix B

Tools for Developing and Implementing an Accountability System

Accountability Indicators and Strategies

Systemwide Accountability Indicators	School-Based Strategy to Support the Systemwide Indicator

Systemwide Accountability Indicators	School-Based Strategy to Support the Systemwide Indicator

Subject Areas and Accountability Indicators

Accountability Area	Indicators (NOT Test Scores)
Language Arts	
Mathematics	
Science	
Social Studies	
Other Areas	

Outline for Discussion of Accountability Report and Next Steps

Agenda Item	Facilitator	Next Steps
1. Strengths—What does the accountability report tell us are the strongest areas for our students? (Review systemwide indicators, including sub-scales of state and district assessments.)		
2. Challenges—What does the accountability report tell us are the most challenging areas for our students?		
3. Strategies in Our School—What do the school-based indicators tell us about the instructional strategies we used that were associated with our achievement results? What inferences can we draw from this? Which strategies were effective? Which strategies were not effective?		

Agenda Item	Facilitator	Next Steps
4. Strategies in Other Schools—Identify some schools that had success in areas where we had challenges. What were the school-based indicators employed by those schools? What can we learn about the strategies that those schools used?		
5. Unnoticed Strategies—What was happening in our school (perhaps revealed in the narrative part of the accountability report) that might have influenced our student achievement? What does this suggest for our school-based goals for next year?		

Appendix C

Contact Information for State Departments of Education and Other Organizations

This appendix contains Web addresses and phone numbers for the departments of education in all 50 states and the District of Columbia and for other organizations with information that may be useful to task forces developing a comprehensive accountability system for a school or a district. As they study other accountability systems, task force members may find that the Internet is a good place to go for the most current information on educational policy. Most of these sites contain information on the state's accountability system, although it may not be referred to in that way. A careful look at the testing, rewards, sanctions, and success indicators mentioned on the site will provide a clue as to how that state holds its stakeholders accountable.

Web Sites	Telephone Numbers
Alabama http://www.alsde.edu	Dept. of Education (334) 242-9700
Alaska http://www.educ.state.ak.us	Dept. of Education (907) 465-2800

Web Sites	Telephone Numbers
Arizona http://www.ade.state.az.us	Dept. of Education (602) 542-3111
Arkansas http://arkedu.state.ar.us	Dept. of Education (501) 682-4475
California http://www.cde.ca.gov	Accountability Assistance (916) 657-3745
California http://www.cresst.org/index1.htm	National Center for Research on Evaluation, Standards, and Student Testing (CRESST) (310) 206-1532
Colorado http://www.cde.state.co.us	Dept. of Education (303) 866-6600
Colorado http://www.ecs.org/	Education Commission of the States (ECS) (303) 299-3600
Connecticut http://www.state.ct.us/sde/	Dept. of Education (860) 566-5677
Delaware http://www.doe.state.de.us	Dept. of Education (302) 739-460
District of Columbia http://www.k12.dc.us	District of Columbia Public Schools (202) 724-4222
District of Columbia http://www.ncela.gwu.edu/	National Clearinghouse for English Language Acquisition & Language Instruction Educational Programs (NCELA) (202) 467-0867 or (800) 321-6223
District of Columbia http://nces.ed.gov/nationsreportcard/	National Center for Education Sta- tistics (NCES) (202) 502-7300
Florida http://www.firn.edu/doe/index.html	Dept. of Education (850) 245-0505
Georgia http://www.doe.k12.ga.us	Dept. of Education (404) 656-2800
Hawaii http://doe.k12.hi.us/	Dept. of Education (808) 586-3230
Idaho http://www.sde.state.id.us/Dept/	Dept. of Education (208) 332-6800
Illinois http://www.isbe.state.il.us	Quality Assurance Office (217) 782-2948
Indiana http://www.doe.state.in.us	Dept. of Education (317) 232-0808

Web Sites	Telephone Numbers
Iowa http://www.state.ia.us/educate	Dept. of Education (515) 281-5294
Kansas http://www.ksbe.state.ks.us	Dept. of Education (785) 296-320
Kentucky http://www.kde.state.ky.us	Director, Assessment/Accountabil- ity Communications (502) 564-3421
Louisiana http://www.doe.state.la.us	Dept. of Education (504) 342-3602
Maine http://www.state.me.us/educa- tion/homepage.htm	Dept. of Education (207) 624-6620
Maryland http://www.msde.state.md.us	Dept. of Education (410) 767-0100 or (888) 246-0016
Massachusetts http://www.doe.mass.edu	Dept. of Education (617) 388-3000
Michigan http://www.michigan.gov/mde	Dept. of Education (517) 373-3324
Minnesota http://www.educ.state.mn.us	Dept. of Children, Families, and Learning (651) 582-8200
Mississippi http://www.mde.k12.ms.us/ ed_accountability/index.html	Dept. of Education, Educational Accountability (601) 359-2038
Missouri http://services.dese.state.mo.us	School Improvement Program (573) 751-4426
Montana http://www.opi.state.mt.us/ index.html	Office of Public Instruction (406) 444-3095 or (888) 231-9393
Nebraska http://www.nde.state.ne.us/	Dept. of Education (402) 471-2295
Nevada http://www.nde.state.nv.us/admin/ super/statebrd/	Dept. of Education (775) 687-9200
New Hampshire http://www.state.nh.us/doe/	Dept. of Education (603) 271-3494
New Jersey http://www.state.nj.us	Dept. of Education (609) 292-4469
New Mexico http://www.sde.state.nm.us	Assessment/Evaluation Unit (505) 827-6524
New York http://www.nysed.gov	Dept. of Education (518) 474-3852

Web Sites	Telephone Numbers
North Carolina http://www.dpi.state.nc.us	Dept. of Public Instruction (919) 807-3300
North Dakota http://www.dpi.state.nd.us	Dept. of Public Instruction (701) 328-2260
Ohio http://www.ode.state.oh.us	Dept. of Education (877) 644-6338
Oklahoma http://sde.state.ok.us	Dept. of Education (405) 521-3301
Oregon http://www.ode.state.or.us	Dept. of Education (503) 378-3569
Pennsylvania http://www.pde.state.pa.us/ stateboard_ed/site/default.asp?g= 0&pde_internetNav=%7C	Dept. of Education (717) 783-6788
Rhode Island http://www.ridoe.net/	Dept. of Education (401) 222-4600
South Carolina http://www.sde.state.sc.us/	Dept. of Education (803) 734-8815
South Dakota http://www.state.sd.us/deca	Office of Technical Assistance (605) 773-6119
Tennessee http://www.state.tn.us/education	Dept. of Education (615) 741-2731
Texas http://www.tea.state.tx.us	Texas Education Agency (512) 463-9734
Utah http://www.usoe.k12.ut.us/eval/	Office of Education (801) 538-7810
Vermont http://www.state.vt.us/educ	Dept. of Education (802) 828-3135
Virginia http://www.pen.k12.va.us	Dept. of Education (804) 225-2020
Washington http://www.k12.wa.us/	Office of Superintendent of Public Instruction (360) 725-6000
West Virginia http://wvde.state.wv.us	Dept. of Education (304) 558-0304
Wisconsin http://www.state.wi.us/ agencies/dpi	Dept. of Public Instruction (800) 441-4563
Wyoming http://www.k12.wy.us/index.htm	Dept. of Education (307) 777-7673

In addition to looking at the accountability information on the Web pages of other states, task force members can also use Internet search engines to locate external resource information. By entering terms such as "educational accountability" or "school accountability" at a search engine prompt, task force members can scan articles and other resources. The following are some Web site addresses that you may find helpful in your search for external accountability information.

- Accountability for Student Learning, Iowa Association of School Boards, http://www.ia-sb.org/services/ableaccountability.asp

- Annenberg Institute for School Reform, http://www.annenberginstitute.org/

- The Center for Education Reform: About Education Reform, http://edreform.com/reform.htm

- Center for Performance Assessment, http://www.MakingStandardsWork.com

- Council of Great City Schools, http://www.cgcs.org

- "Creating Accountability in Big City Schools," an article by Linda Darling-Hammond and Carol Ascher, http://eric-web.tc.columbia.edu/mono/UDS102.pdf

- Emerging Student Assessment Systems for School Reform, http://www.ed.gov/databases/ERIC_Digests/ed389959.html

- Focus on Accountability, http://www.aacte.org/accreditation_issues/focus_basic_value.htm

- Framework for Educational Accountability, http://education.umn.edu/NCEO/Framework/framework.html

- Issues in Education Websites, http://www.stf.sk.ca/teaching_res/research/issues_in_educ.htm

- National Center on Educational Outcomes, http://education.umn.edu/nceo/

- NEA (National Education Association) Issues, http://www.nea.org/issues/
- Occidental College Library, http://oasys.lib.oxy.edu/search/educational+accountability
- Standards and Assessments, http://www.ccsso.org/ standards-assessments.html
- State Education Accountability Systems, Council of Chief State School Officers, http://www.ccsso.org/introprofile.html
- U.S. Department of Education Publications, http://www.ed.gov/pubs/
- Western Regional Resource Center, Inclusive Large Scale Assessment, http://interact.uoregon.edu/ wrrc/assessmentnew.htm

References

Buckingham M., & Clifton, D. O. (2001). *Now discover your strengths: The revolutionary program that shows you how to develop your unique talents and strengths—and those of the people you manage.* New York: Simon & Schuster.

Calkins, L. M. (1983). *Lessons from a child: On the teaching and learning of writing.* Portsmouth, NH: Heinemann.

Calkins, L. M. (1994). *The art of teaching writing* (2nd ed.). *Portsmouth, NH: Heinemann.*

Christenson, D. D. (2001, December). Building state assessment from the classroom up: Why Nebraska has forsworn high-stakes testing in favor of district-tailored measures. *The School Administrator, 58*(11), 27–31.

Coffman, C., Gonzalez Molina, G., & Clifton, J. K. (2002). *Follow this path: How the world's greatest organizations drive growth by unleashing human potential.* New York: Simon & Schuster.

Collins, J. (2001). *Good to great: Why some companies make the leap . . . and others don't.* New York: HarperCollins Publishers, Inc.

Darling-Hammond, L. (1997). *The right to learn: A blueprint for creating schools that work.* San Francisco: Jossey-Bass.

Darling-Hammond, L., & Sykes, G. (1999). *Teaching as the learning profession: Handbook of policy and practice.* San Francisco: Jossey-Bass.

Foersterling, F., & Morgenstern, M. (2002). Accuracy of self-assessment and task performance: Does it pay to know the truth? *Journal of Educational Psychology, 94*(3), 576–585.

Goleman, D. (1998). *Working with emotional intelligence.* New York: Bantam Books.

Goleman, D., Boyatzis, R., & McKee, A. (2002). *Primal leadership: Realizing the power of emotional intelligence.* Boston: Harvard Business School Press.

Goodnough, A., & Medina, J. (2003, February 14). Klein reveals how he chose top schools [electronic version]. *New York Times,* retrieved March 17, 2002, from http://query.nytimes.com/search/restricted/article?res=F60F17F73E5E0C778DDDAB0894DB404482

Ingersoll, R. M. (2003, January 7). To close the gap, quality counts. *Education Week,* 7–18.

Ingersoll, R. M., & Smith, T. M. (2003, May). The wrong solution to the teacher shortage. *Educational Leadership, 60*(8), 30-33.

Jerald, C. D. (2001). *Dispelling the myth revisited: Preliminary findings from a nationwide analysis of "high-flying" schools.* Washington, DC: The Education Trust, Inc.

Marzano, R. J. (2003). *What works in schools: Translating research into action.* Alexandria, VA: Association for Supervision and Curriculum Development.

Marzano, R. J., Pickering, D. J. & Pollock, J. E. (2001). *Classroom instruction that works: Research-based strategies for increasing student achievement.* Alexandria, VA: Association for Supervision and Curriculum Development.

Ohanian, S. (1999). *One size fits few: The folly of educational standards.* Portsmouth, NH: Heinemann.

Pfeffer, J., &. Sutton, R. I. (2000). *The knowing-doing gap: How smart companies turn knowledge into action.* Boston: Harvard Business School Press.

Reeves, D. B. (2000a). *Accountability in action: A blueprint for learning organizations.* Denver, CO: Advanced Learning Press.

Reeves, D. B. (2000b). Standards are not enough: Essential transformations for successful schools. *NASSP Bulletin, 84*(620), 5–19.

Reeves, D. B. (2001a). *Crusade in the classroom: How George W. Bush's education reforms will affect your children, our schools.* New York: Simon & Schuster.

Reeves, D. B. (2001b, June 6). If you hate standards, learn to love the bell curve. *Education Week,* 48.

Reeves, D. B. (featured presenter) (2001c). *Accountability for greater student learning* [videotape]. East Sandy, UT: Video Journal of Education.

Reeves, D. B. (2002a). *The daily disciplines of leadership: How to improve student achievement, staff motivation, and personal organization.* San Francisco: Jossey-Bass.

Reeves, D. B. (2002b). *Holistic accountability: Serving students, schools, and community*. Thousand Oaks, CA: Corwin Press.

Reeves, D. B. (2002c). *The leader's guide to standards: A blueprint for educational equity and excellence*. San Francisco: Jossey-Bass.

Reeves, D. B. (2002d). *Making standards work: How to implement standards-based performance assessments in the classroom, school, and district* (3rd ed). Denver, CO: Advanced Learning Press.

Reeves, D. B. (2002e). *Reason to write: Help your child succeed in school and in life through better reasoning and clear communication*. New York: Kaplan.

Reeves, D. B. (2003a). *Assessing educational leaders: Evaluating performance for improved individual and organizational results*. Thousand Oaks, CA: Corwin Press.

Reeves, D. B. (2003b). *Power standards, unwrapping the standards, and making standards work*. Denver, CO: Advanced Learning Press.

Reeves, D. B., & Brandt, R. (2003, January/February). Point-counterpoint: Take back the standards. *Leadership, 32*(3), 16–21.

Sanders, W. L. (1998, December). Value-added assessment: A method for measuring the effects of the system, school and teacher on the rate of student academic progress [electronic version]. *The School Administrator,* retrieved March 5, 2003, from http://www.aasa.org/publications/sa/1998_12/contents.htm

Simpson, J. O. (2003, January). Beating the odds. *American School Board Journal, 190*(1), 43–47.

Stevenson, H. W., & Stigler, J. W. (1992*). The teaching gap: Why our schools are failing and what we can learn from Japanese and Chinese education*. New York: Simon & Schuster.

Stiggins, R. J. (2001). *Student-involved classroom assessment* (3rd ed.). Upper Saddle River, NJ: Prentice Hall.

Thomas, K. W. (2002). *Intrinsic motivation at work: Building energy and commitment*. San Francisco: Berrett-Koehler Publishers, Inc.

United States Department of Education. (2002, July 5). Title I, Improving the academic achievement of the disadvantaged, 34 C.F.R part 200.

Index

About the Author

Douglas Reeves leads the Center for Performance Assessment, an international organization dedicated to improving student achievement and educational equity. Through its long-term relationships with school systems, the Center helps educators and school leaders with practical and constructive approaches to standards, assessment, and accountability.

Dr. Reeves is a frequent keynote speaker in the United States and abroad for education, government, and business organizations and is a faculty member of leadership programs sponsored by the Harvard Graduate School of Education. He is the author of 17 books, including the best-selling *Making Standards Work,* now in its third edition. Other recent titles include *The Daily Disciplines of Leadership: How to Improve Student Achievement, Staff Motivation, and Personal Organization* (Jossey-Bass, 2002); *The Leader's Guide to Standards: A Blueprint for Educational Equity and Excellence* (Jossey-Bass, 2002); and *Reason to Write: Help Your Child Succeed in School and in Life Through Better Reasoning and Clear Communication* (Kaplan, 2002). His books have twice been selected for the Harvard Distinguished Authors Series, and his writing for parents and children won the Parents' Choice award for 2002.

Beyond his work in large-scale assessment and research, Dr. Reeves has devoted many years to classroom teaching with students ranging from elementary school to doctoral candidates. His family includes four children ranging from elementary school through college age, all of whom have attended public schools. His wife, Shelley Sackett, is an attorney, mediator, and school board member. He lives near Boston and can be reached at dreeves@MakingStandardsWork.com, or:

Center for Performance Assessment

Massachusetts: 781-477-1880 Fax: 781-477-0231

Colorado: 800-844-6599 or 303-504-9312

     Fax: 303-504-9417

http://www.MakingStandardsWork.com